RECORDED VERSIONS
GUITAR

AUTHENTIC TRANSCRIPTIONS
WITH NOTES AND TABLATURE

JIMI HENDRIX • LIVE AT THE ISLE OF WIGHT

BLUE WILD ANGEL

Music transcriptions by Andy Aledort

Cover photo: Chris Walter/Authentic Hendrix L.L.C.

ISBN 0-634-05728-6

EXPERIENCE
HENDRIX™

EXCLUSIVELY DISTRIBUTED BY

HAL•LEONARD®
CORPORATION
7777 W. BLUEMOUND RD. P.O. BOX 13819 MILWAUKEE, WI 53213

Visit Hal Leonard Online at
www.halleonard.com

The Queen
(Adaptation of "God Save the Queen")
Words and Music by Jimi Hendrix

*"Yeah! Thank you very much for showing up, man. You all look really beautiful and outtasite, and thanks for waiting.
It has been a long time, hasn't it? [flashes "peace sign" to the crowd] That does mean "peace," not this [reverse
"peace sign"]. Peace! Ok, give us about a minute to tune up, alright? Give us...give us about a minute to tune up."
[Band readies their instruments and Jimi plays a few licks.] "It's so good to be back in England. We'd like to do,
uh, start off with a thing that everybody knows out there. You could join in, start singing...matter-of-fact, it would
sound better if you'd stand up for your country and your beliefs and start singing. And if you don't, fuck you." [laughter]
[to band] "Nice and loud, nice and loud."*

Tune down 1/2 step:
(low to high) E♭-A♭-D♭-G♭-B♭-E♭

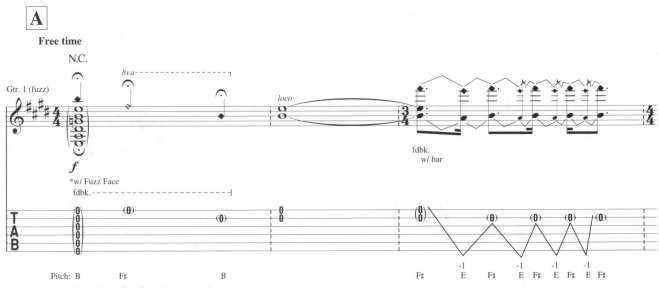

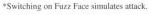

*Switching on Fuzz Face simulates attack.

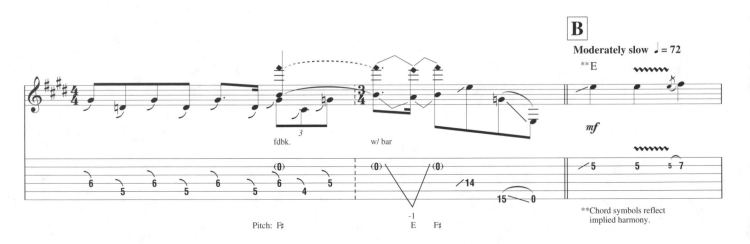

**Chord symbols reflect implied harmony.

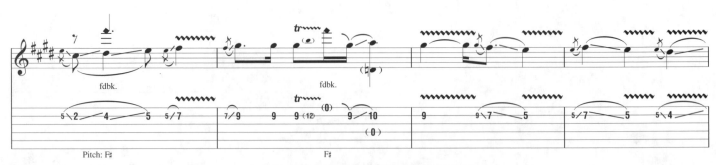

*w/ wah-wah – –

*Rock wah-wah back & forth
as fast as possible.

Freely

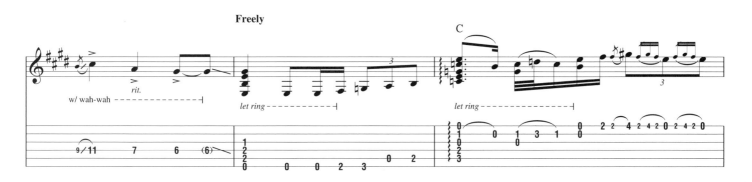

let ring

let ring

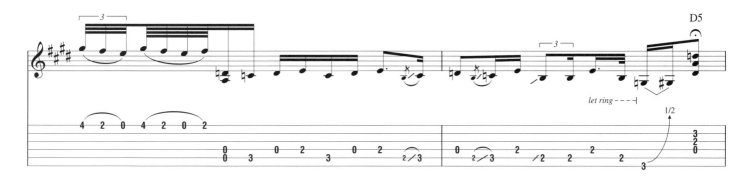

let ring

*Segue to "Sgt. Pepper's Lonely
Hearts Club Band"*

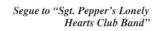

Faster ♩ = 116
Gtr. 1: w/ random fdbk.

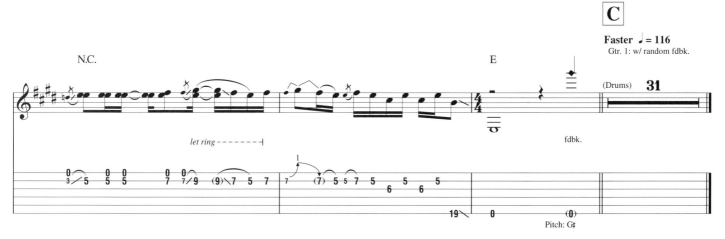

let ring

fdbk.

(Drums) **31**

Pitch: G♯

Sgt. Pepper's Lonely Hearts Club Band

Words and Music by John Lennon and Paul McCartney

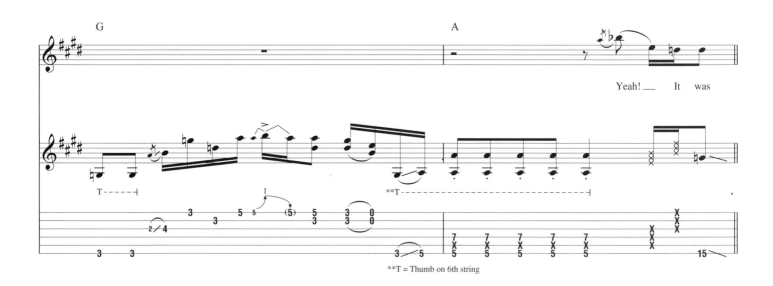

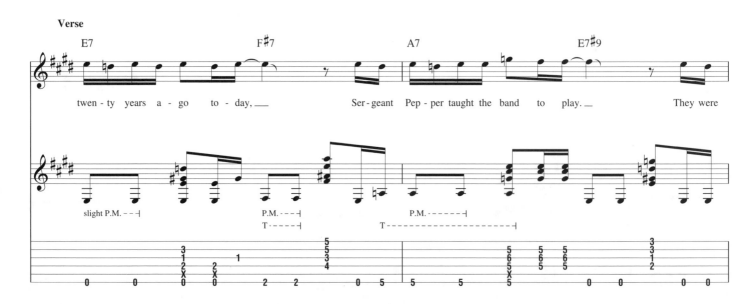

go - in' in and out of style, _____ you know, but here's a, make you smile. ___ So

may I in - tro - duce to you __ the one and on - ly Bill - y Shears. _

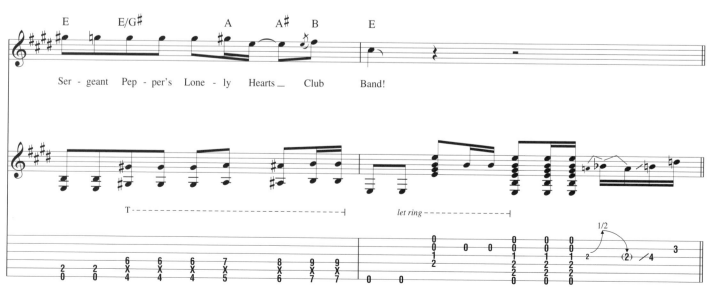

Ser - geant Pep - per's Lone - ly Hearts _ Club Band!

Guitar Solo

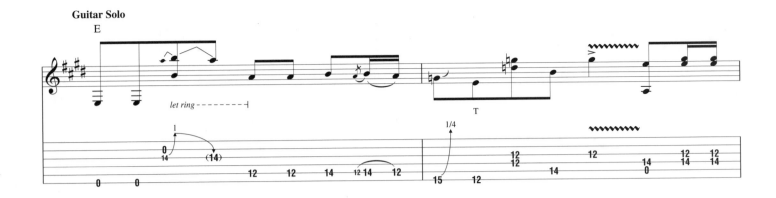

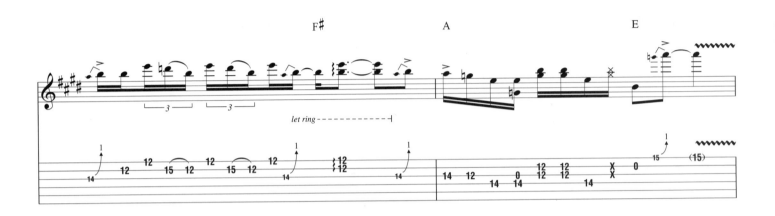

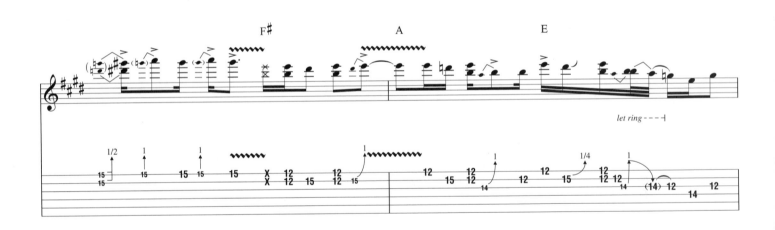

Segue to "Spanish Castle Magic"

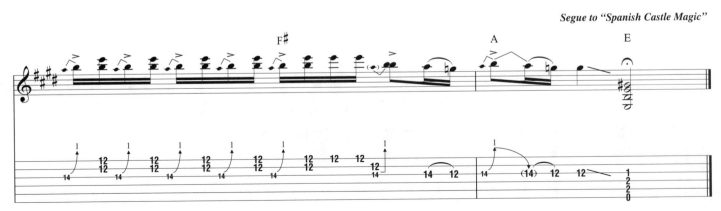

Spanish Castle Magic
Words and Music by Jimi Hendrix

Tune down 1/2 step:
(low to high) E♭-A♭-D♭-G♭-B♭-E♭

Intro

Moderate Rock ♩ = 108

*Chord symbols reflect basic harmony.

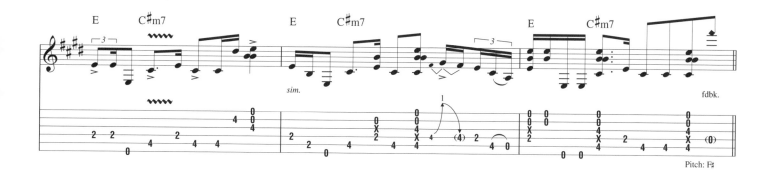

Verse

1. It's ver-y far a-way,   takes a-bout a half a day to

round.   But it's all in your mind, ba - by,   don't waste your time ___ think - in' a - bout

bad things.   Think if I talk to you I'll   *Spoken:* turn your mind a - round!

Chorus

Hang ___ on, my dar - ling,   hang on if you wan-na go.

Spoken: Talk a-bout,   go tell your moth-er 'bout a,   I'm gon-na turn her on!

C#m7

C#m7

Span - ish Cas - tle mag - ic. _____

let ring - - - - - - -

grad. bend

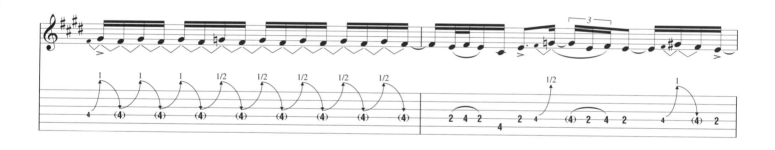

grad. bend

let ring - ⌐

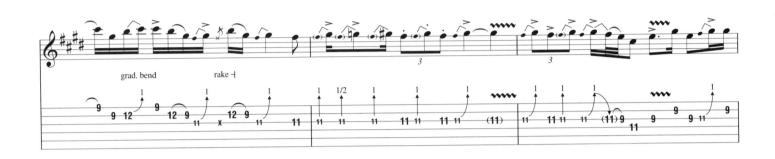

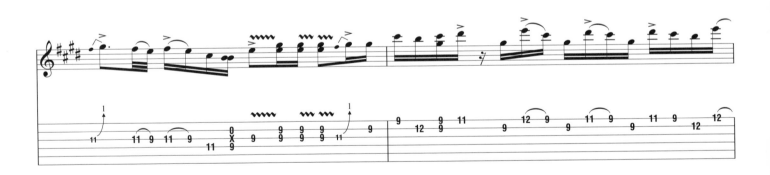

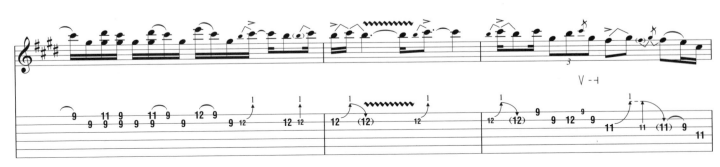

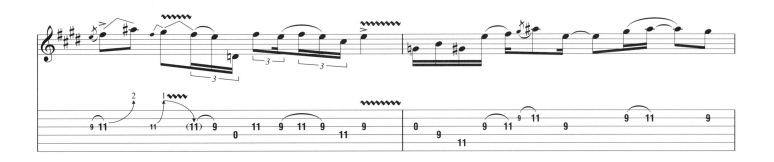

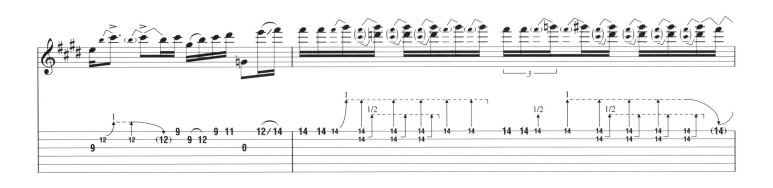

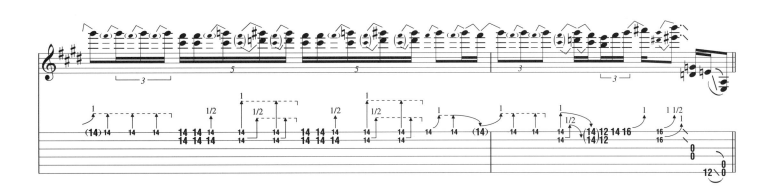

Chorus

Hang — on, my dar - ling,   hang on ___ if you wan-na go.

G#m

We're gon - na... _ *Spoken:* whole lot - ta fun, ba - by!

grad. bend

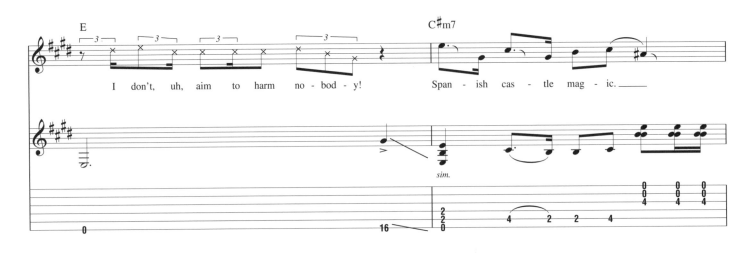

E

C#m7

I don't, uh, aim to harm no - bod - y! Span - ish cas - tle mag - ic. _

sim.

let ring

Lit - tle bit of Span - ish cas - tle mag - ic.

Spoken: It's all in your mind, _ ba - by!

Al - right, __ yeah!   A lit - tle bit here and there ain't nev - er killed no - bod - y.

It's bet - ter than Co - ca Co - la!

Outro-Guitar Solo

C#m7

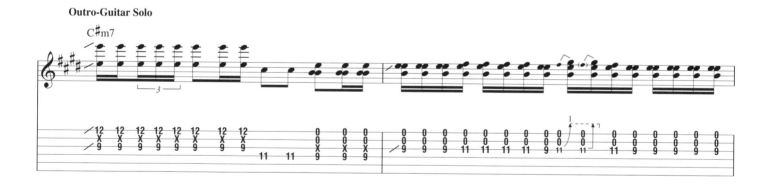

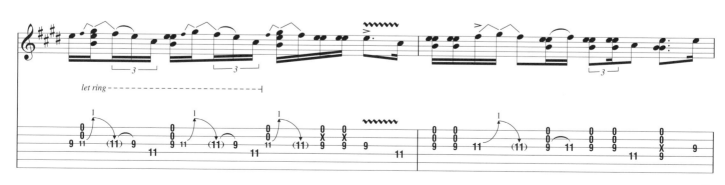

*T

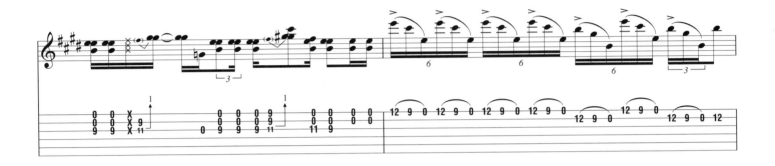

*T = Thumb on 6th string

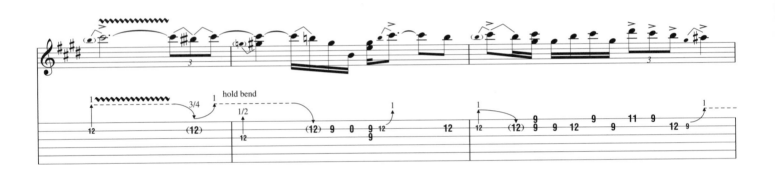

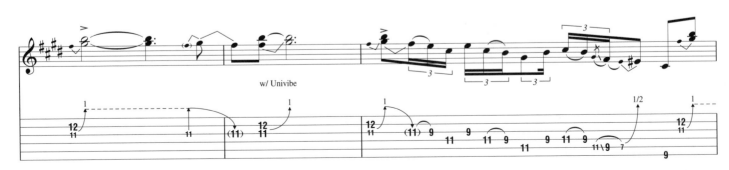

w/ Univibe

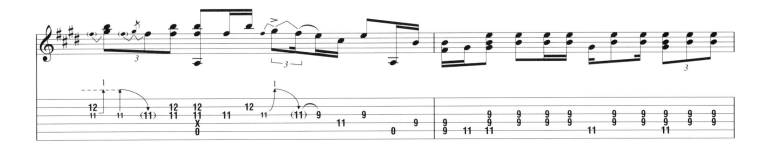

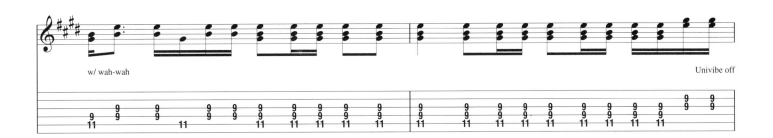

w/ wah-wah

Univibe off

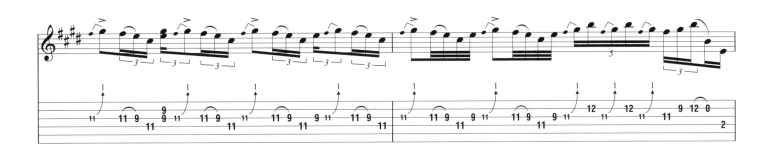

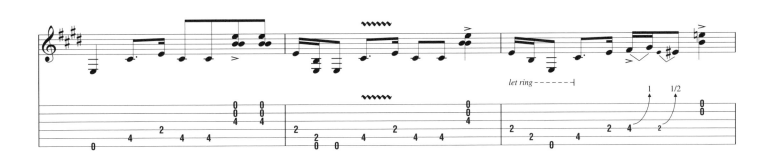

let ring -------|

Free time

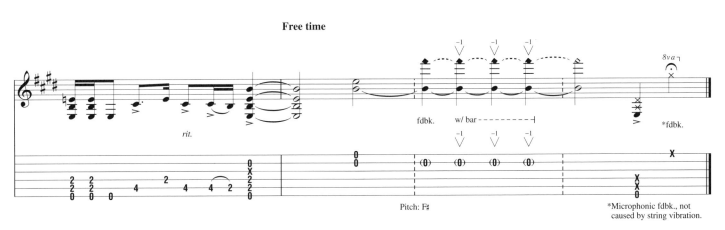

rit.

fdbk.   w/ bar -------|

8va

*fdbk.

Pitch: F#

*Microphonic fdbk., not
caused by string vibration.

All Along the Watchtower

Words and Music by Bob Dylan

Tune down 1/2 step:
(low to high) Eb-Ab-Db-Gb-Bb-Eb

Intro
Moderate Rock ♩ = 120

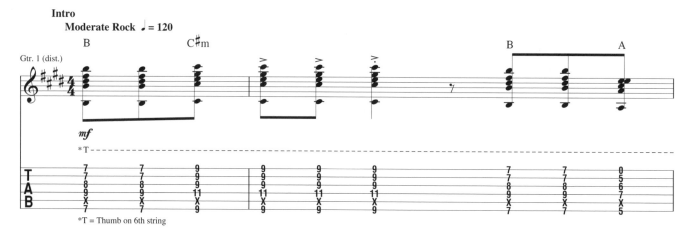

*T = Thumb on 6th string

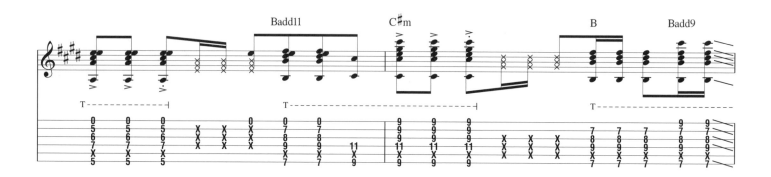

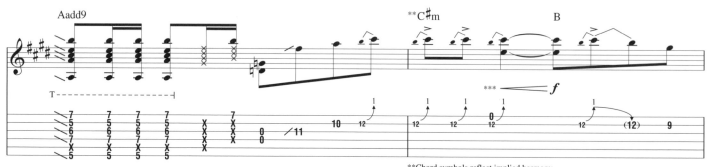

**Chord symbols reflect implied harmony.
***Change dynamic w/ vol. knob.

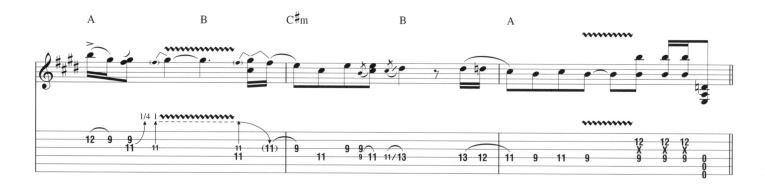

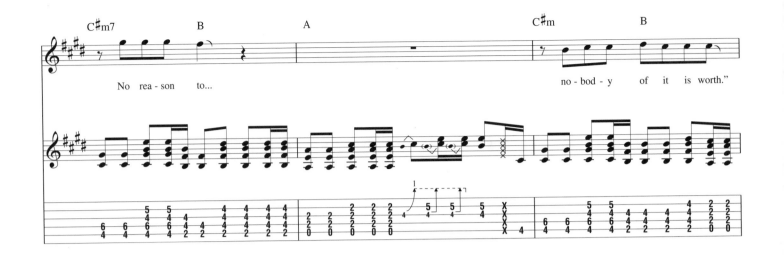

No rea-son to... nobod-y of it is worth."

Guitar Solo

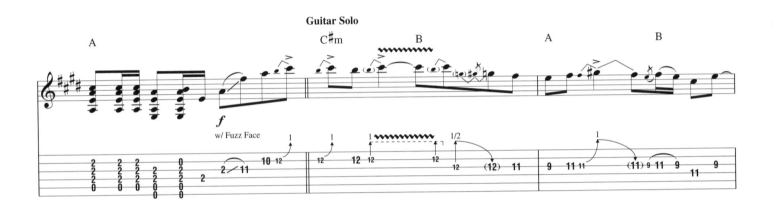

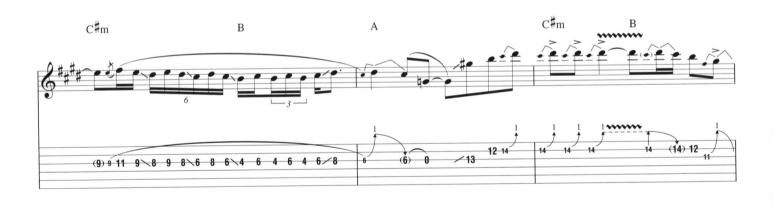

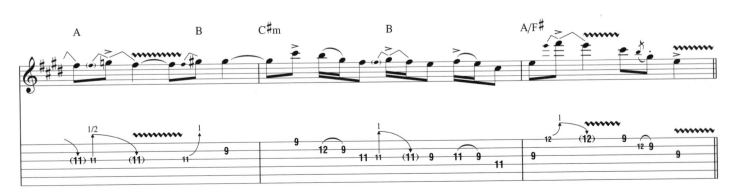

So let us stop _ talk - in' false - ly now, _ the hour's get - ting _ late." _

Guitar Solo

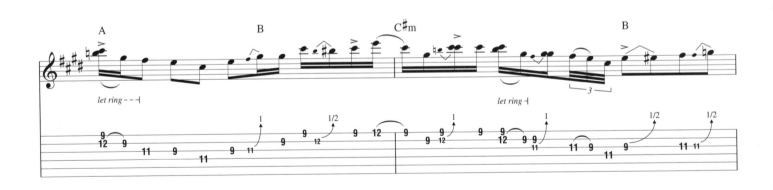

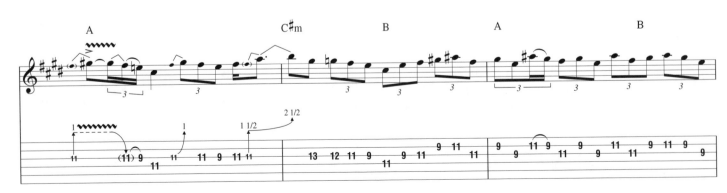

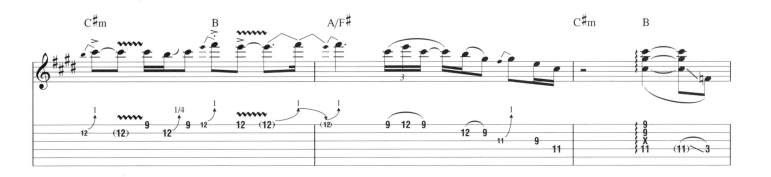

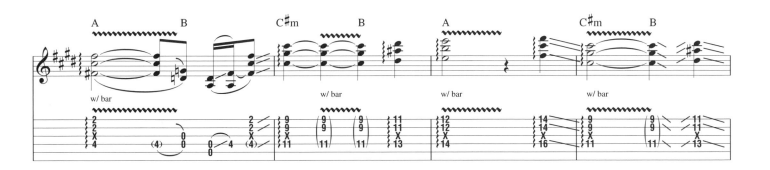

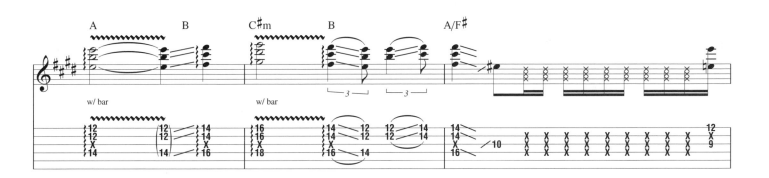

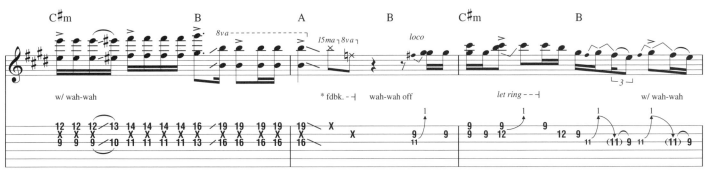

*Microphonic fdbk., not caused by string vibration.

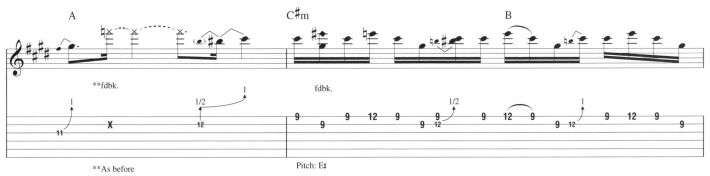

25

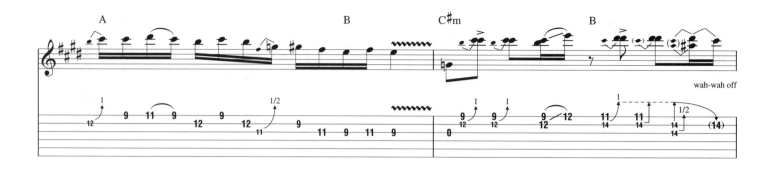

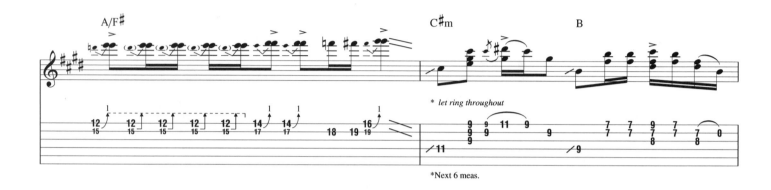

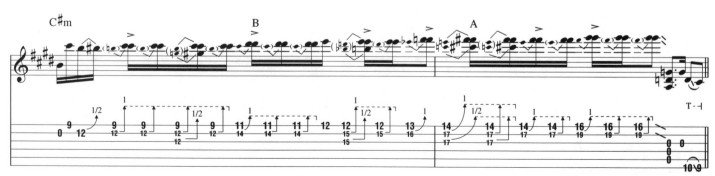

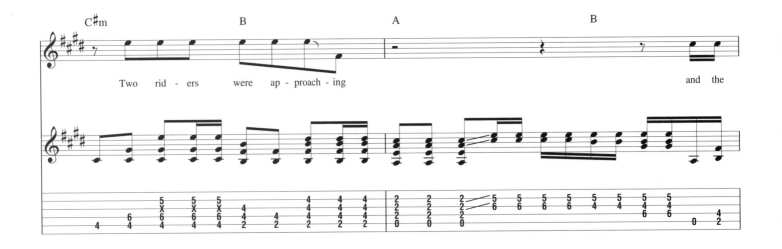

Two rid - ers were ap - proach - ing and the

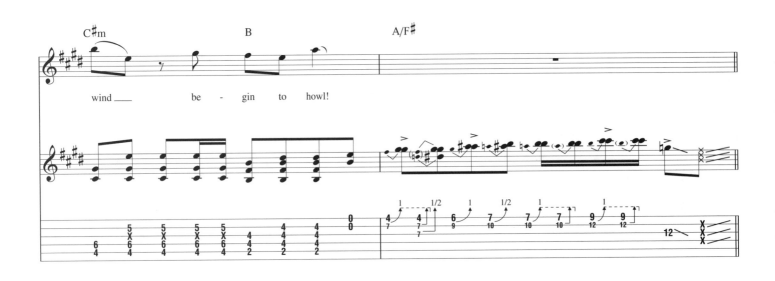

wind ____ be - gin to howl!

Outro-Guitar Solo

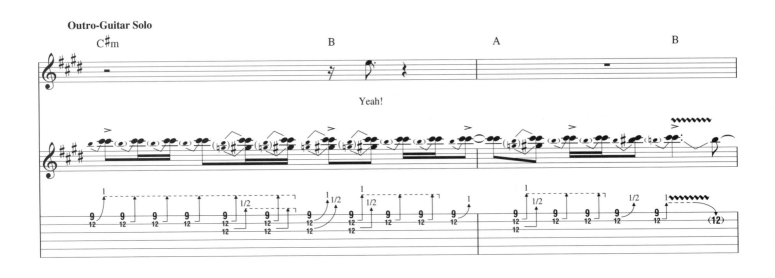

Yeah!

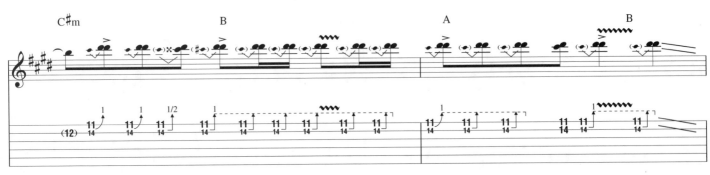

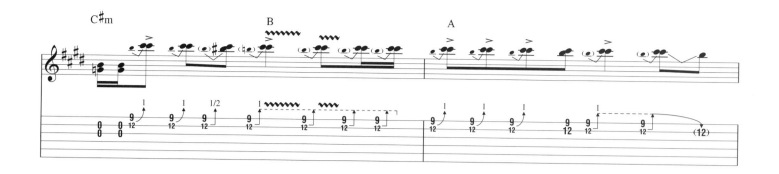

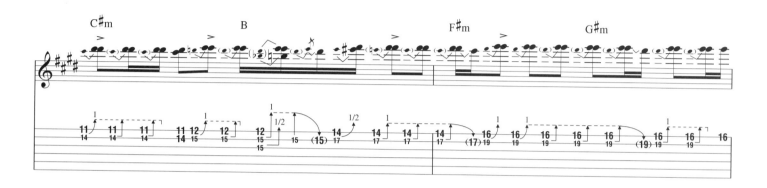

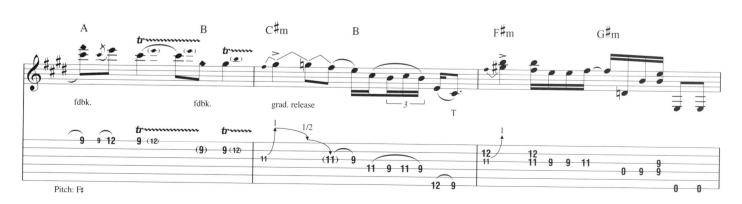

Pitch: F#

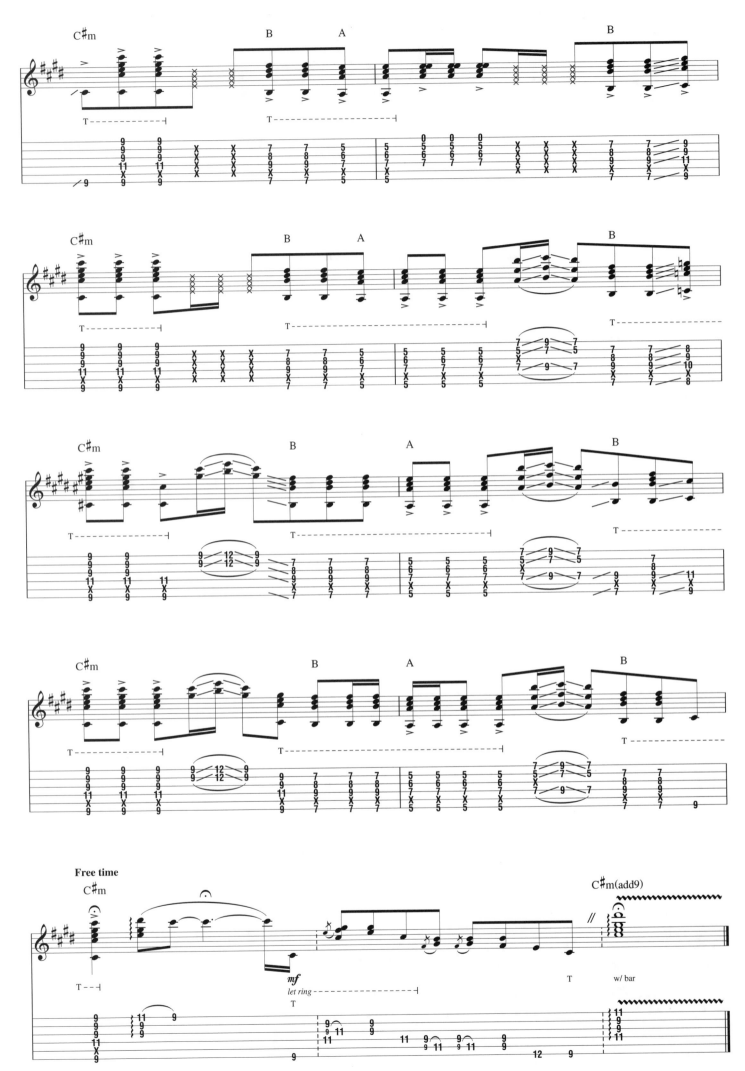

Machine Gun

Words and Music by Jimi Hendrix

"Uh, we're havin' a tiny bit of trouble with the equipment. Hold on one, one more second; buy your hotdogs or whatever.
[Someone yells out "Voodoo Child"] Yeah, we'll do that, uh, towards the, um, the next time. [Jimi checks his tuning and Uni-Vibe settings]

"Yeah, there's a whole lotta head games going on sometimes, and sometimes they leak out, as a word they use their powers
and so forth and play their own head games on other people, which we call WAR... [makes clicking sounds with his mouth].
And so we'd like to dedicate this one to, uh, all the soldiers that are fighting in Birmingham, all the skinheads, all the, uh... yeah,
well, you know what I mean, you know. Yeah, right, amen. All the soldiers fighting in Bournemouth, London... oh yes, all the
soldiers fighting in Viet Nam, I almost forgot, man... so many wars going on."

Tune down 1/2 step:
(low to high) Eb-Ab-Db-Gb-Bb-Eb

Intro
Slow Rock ♩ = 69

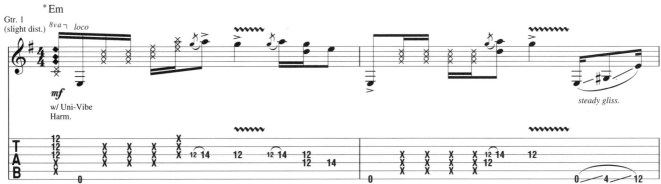

*Chord symbols reflect basic harmony.

**T = Thumb on 6th string

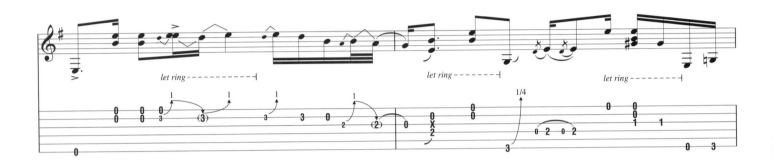

E7#9

*Vibrato achieved by pushing down on string behind nut.

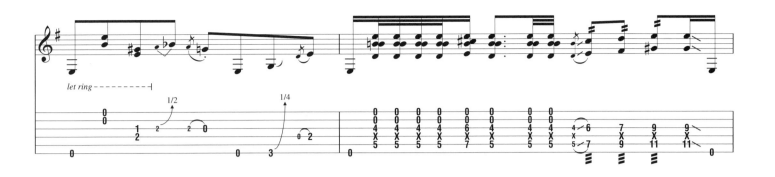

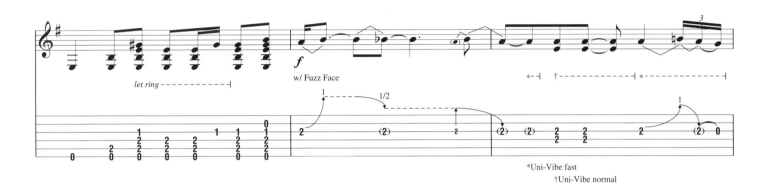

*Uni-Vibe fast
†Uni-Vibe normal

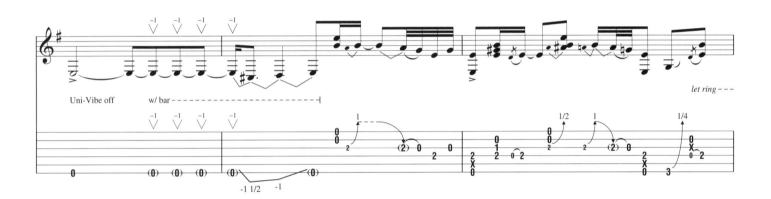

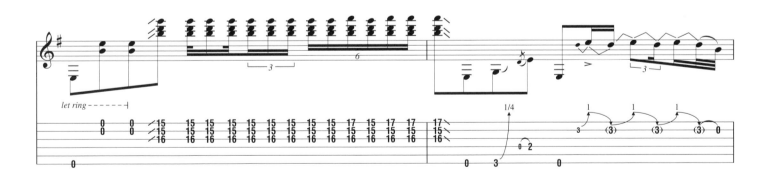

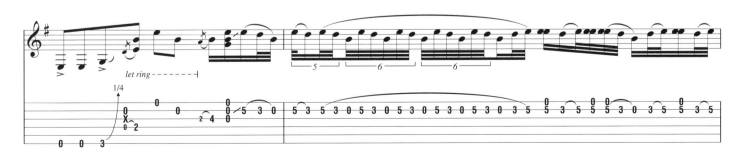

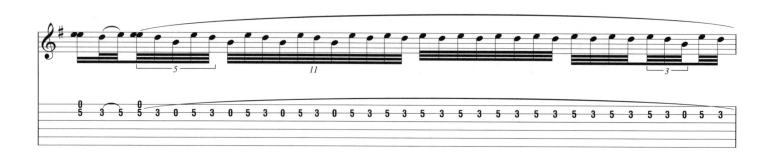

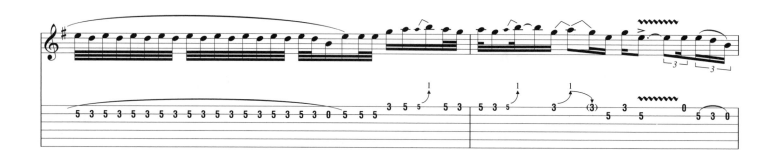

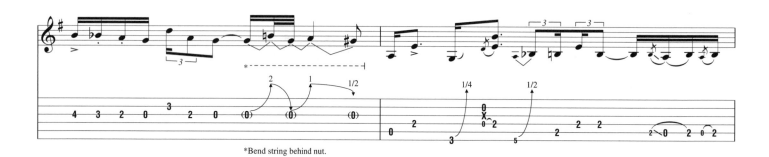

*Bend string behind nut.

grad. bend

let ring

*Open strings sound due to sympathetic vibration.

*w/ radio (VHF) interference.

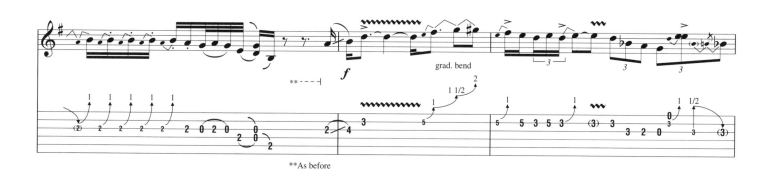

**As before

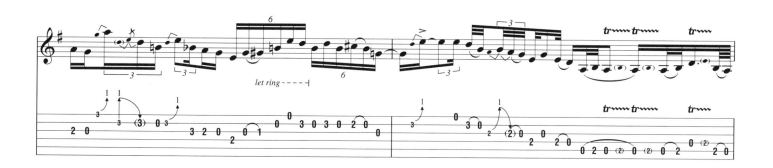

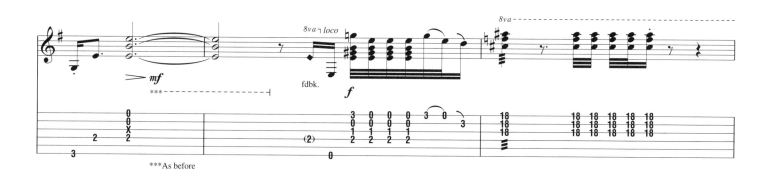

***As before

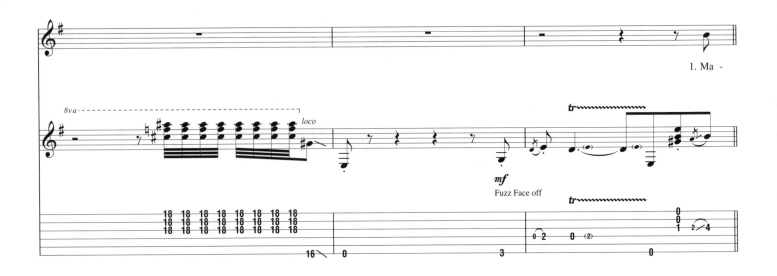

1. Ma -

Verse

E7#9

chine gun,_____   tear - in'_____   my bod-y 'n' soul   a - part!

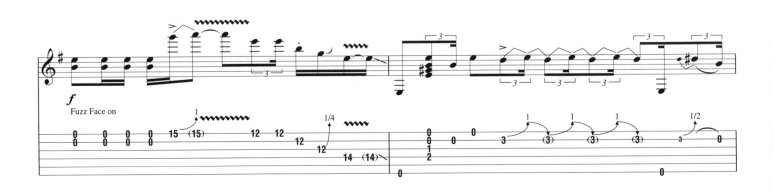

*Flip pickup selector switch rapidly between neck and bridge pickups.

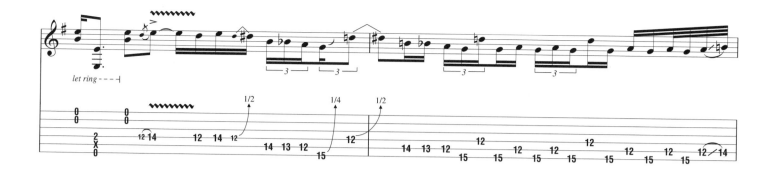

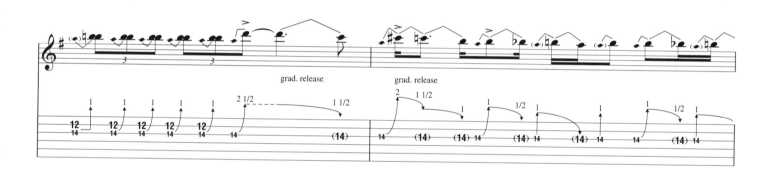

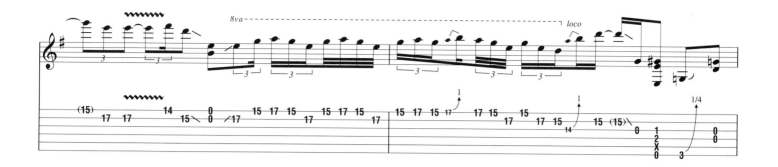

You shoot me down, make me kill you, ba - by! Gon - na make, make me

kill you! E - vil man _ make _ me kill ya!

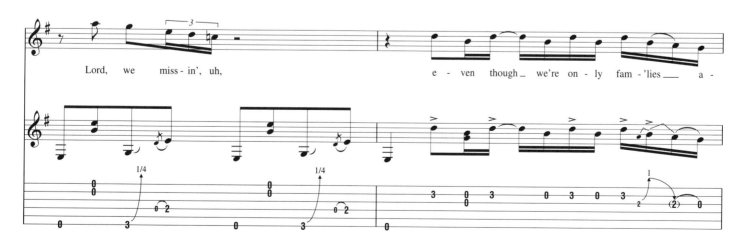

Lord, we miss - in', uh, e - ven though _ we're on - ly fam - 'lies _ a -

Guitar Solo

E7#9

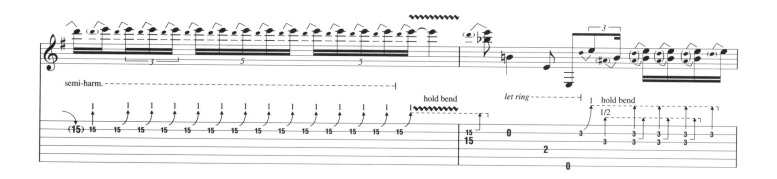

*Jimi quickly flicks ground switch on amplifier back and forth.

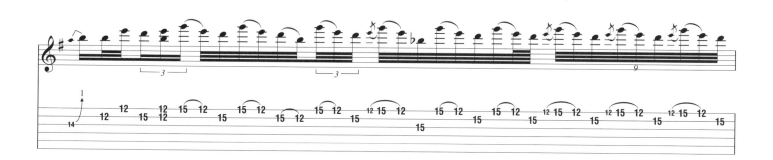

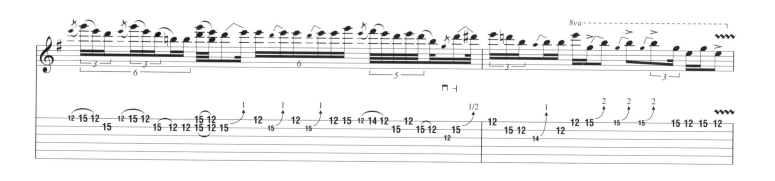

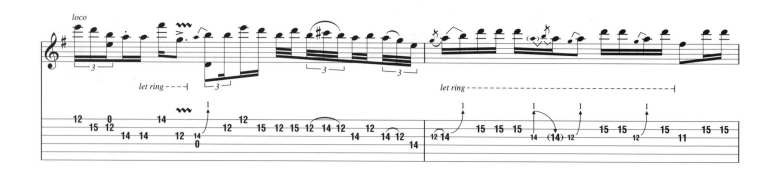

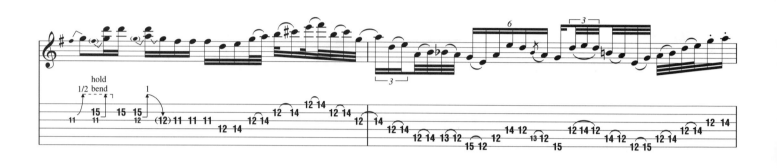

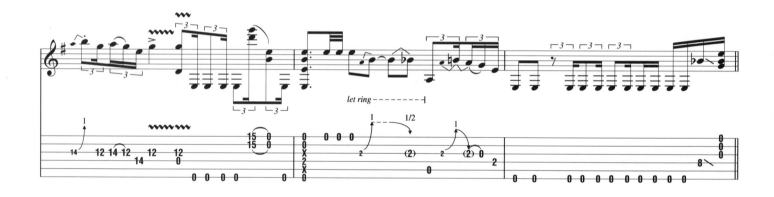

Interlude

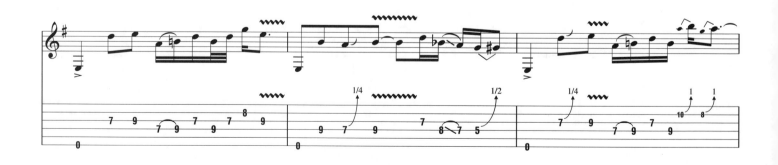

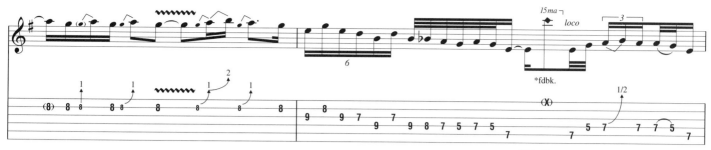

Pitch: C

*Microphonic fdbk., not caused by string vibration.

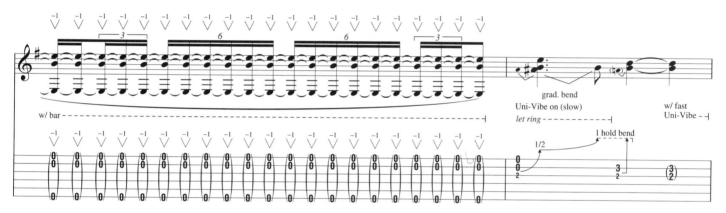

**High E and B strings ring from
sympathetic vibration.

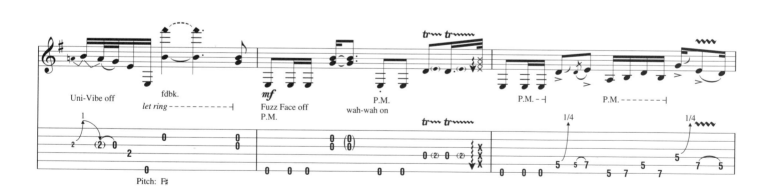

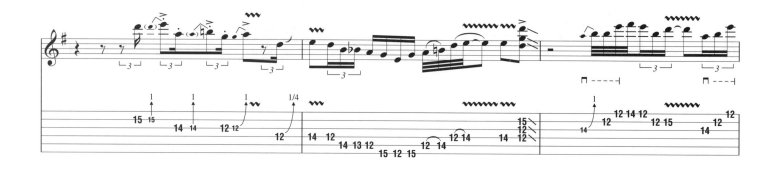

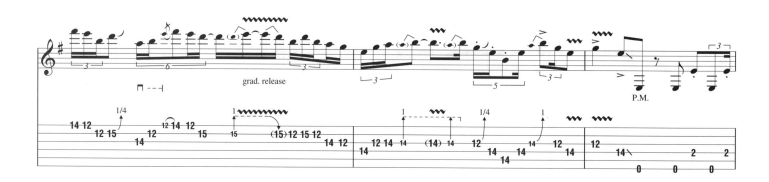

*Bends and vibrato executed by pushing down on third string behind nut.

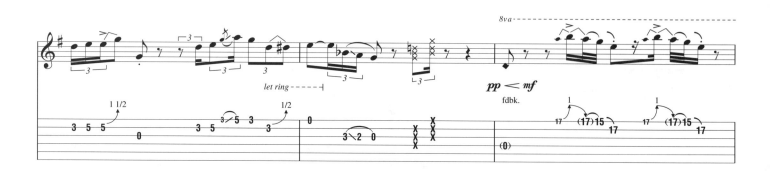

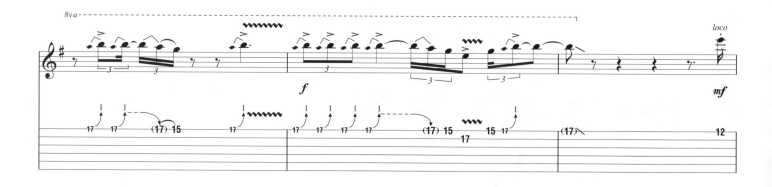

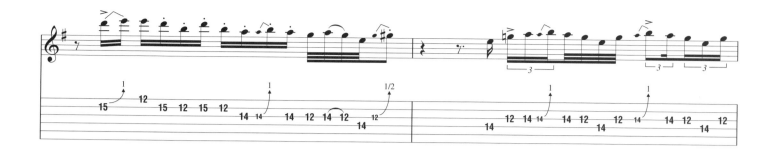

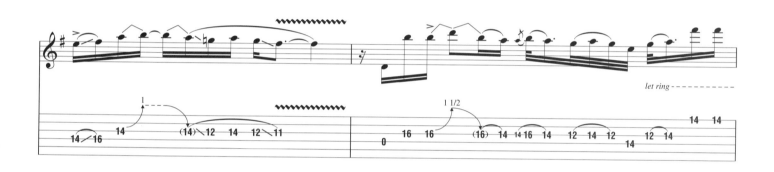

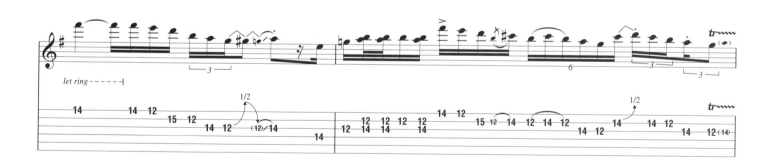

fdbk.   *   w/ bar

Pitch: G#

-1   -1 1/2

*Pick springs in tremolo cavity.

Free time   **Drum Solo**

N.C.   (2:20)

***(42 sec.)

**   ***w/ random pick scrapes & slides.

**Approx. 20 sec.;
Jimi starts & stops randomly.

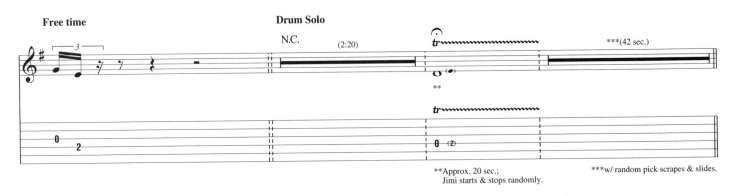

Guitar Solo
In time ♩ = 76   ♩. = 76

Em7

(Drums)

let ring ┥

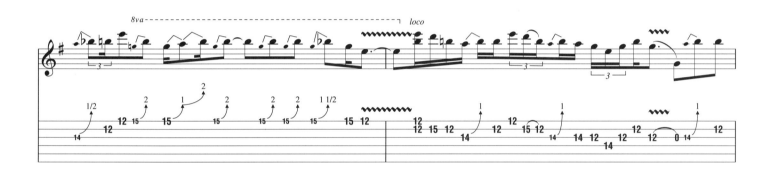

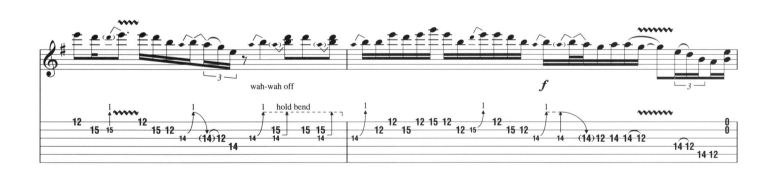

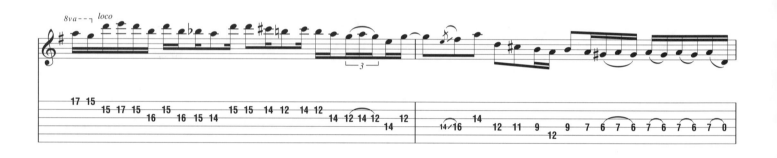

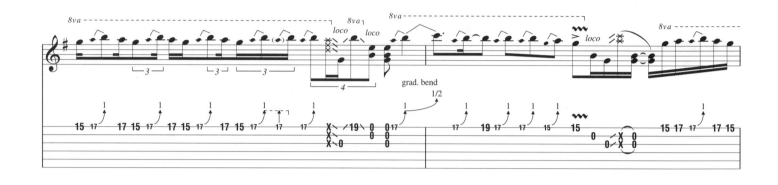

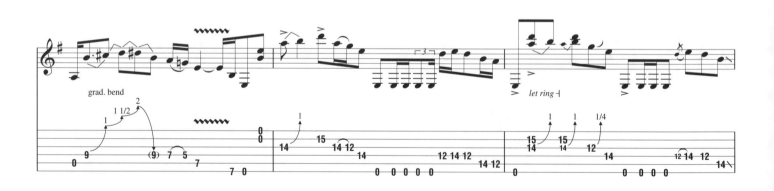

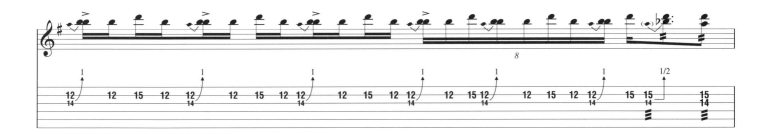

Interlude

($\cdot = \cdot$)

Em7

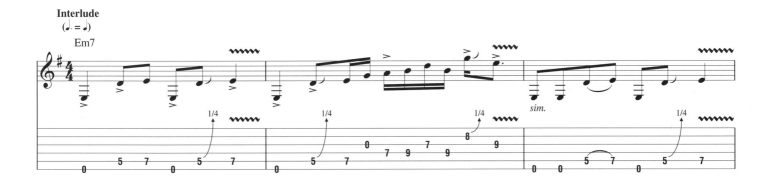

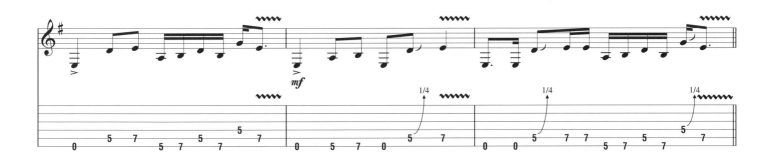

Verse

Em7

2. Well, I pick up my axe an' fight like a farm - er,

fdbk.

Pitch: F♯

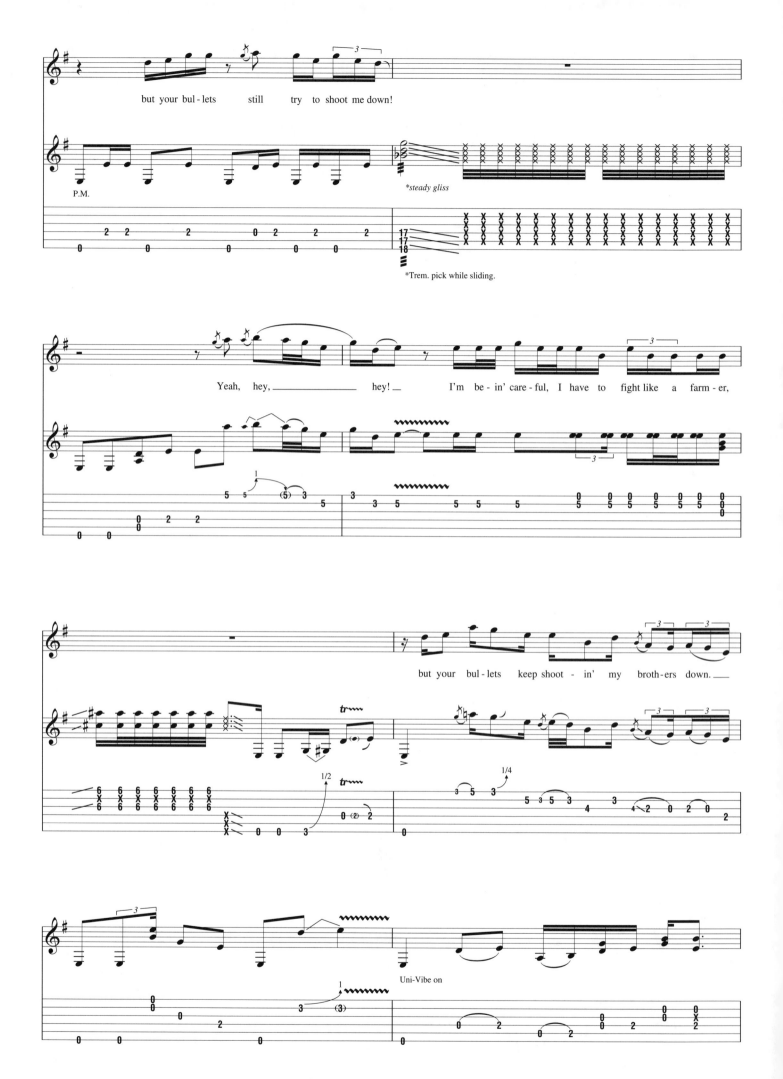

Same way you shoot me down, ba-by, you'll be go-in' just the same, three times the pain, and your own self to blame! Hey, hey, ma-chine gun!

Guitar Solo

Em7

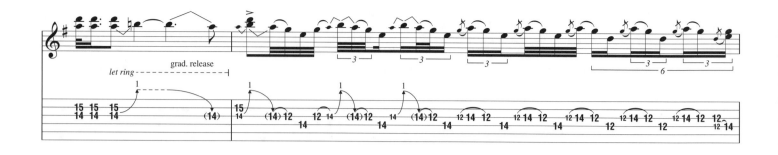

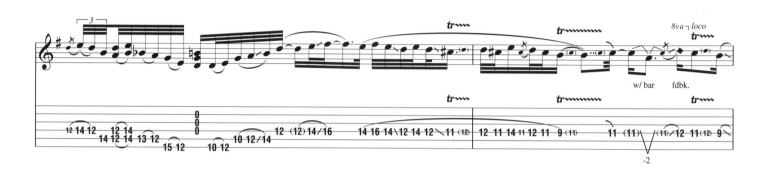

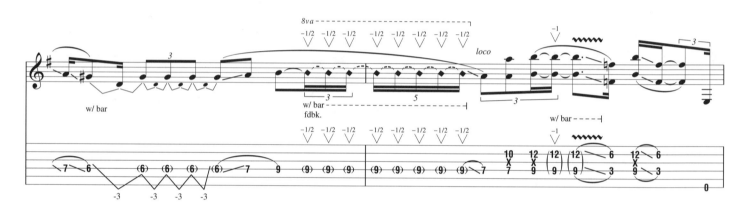

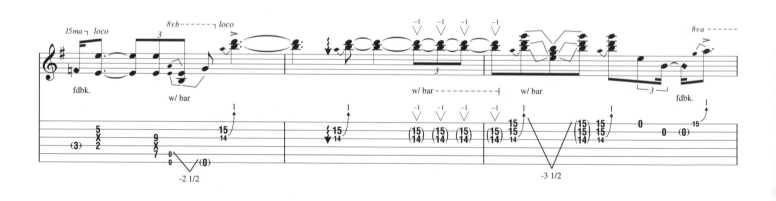

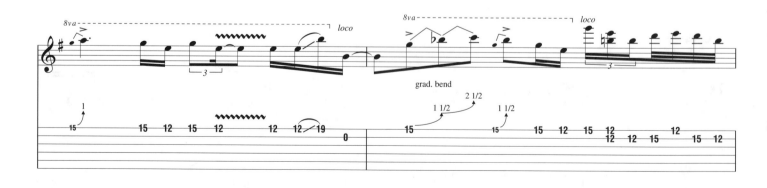

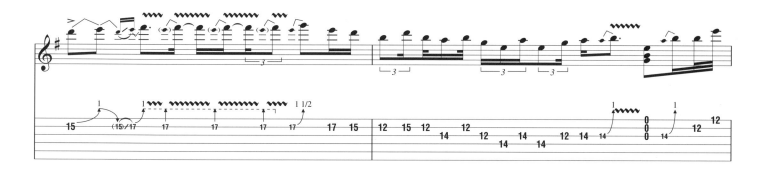

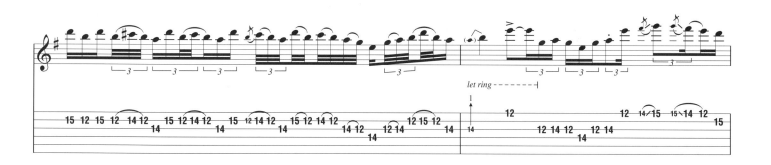

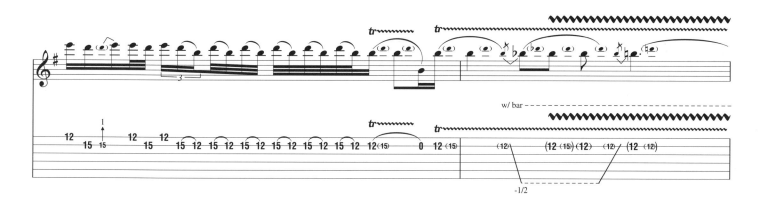

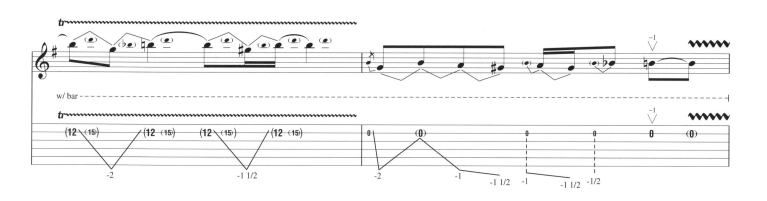

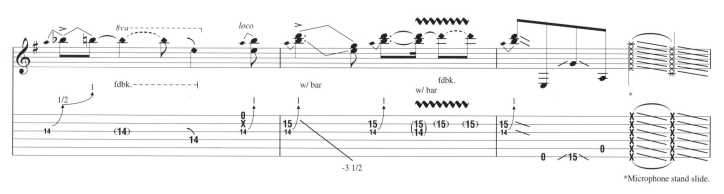

*Microphone stand slide.

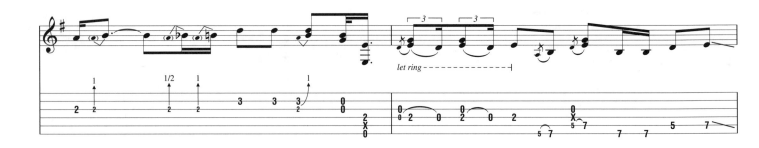

E

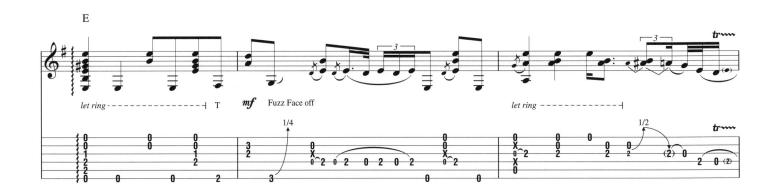

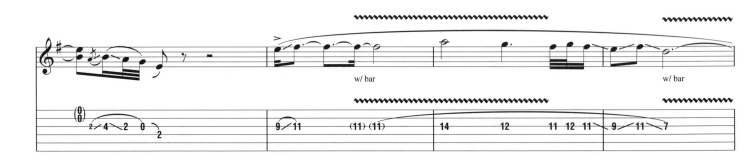

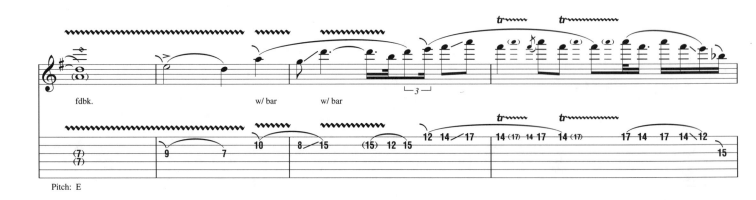

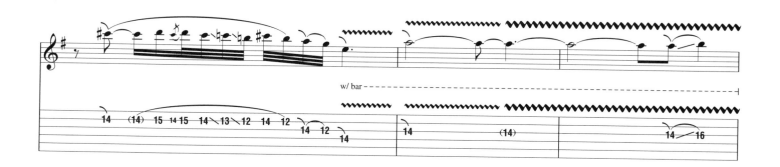

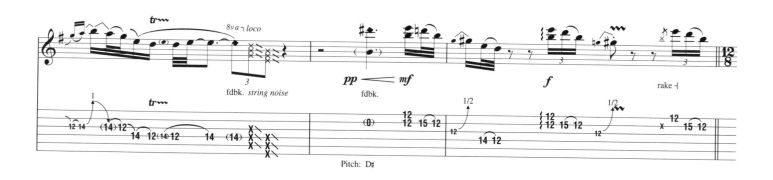

Interlude
Faster ♩ = 144

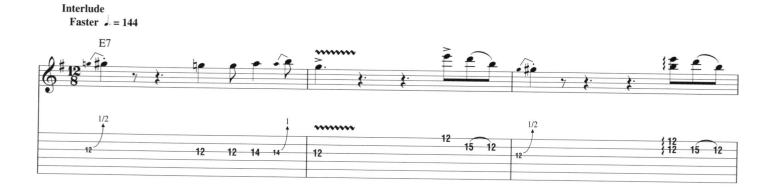

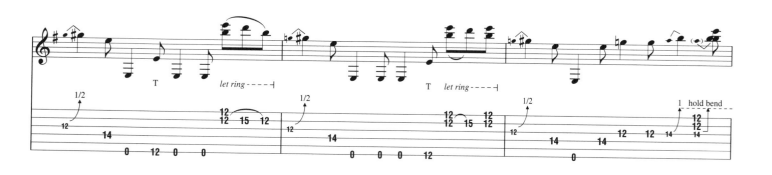

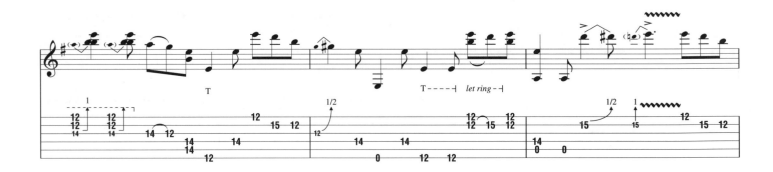

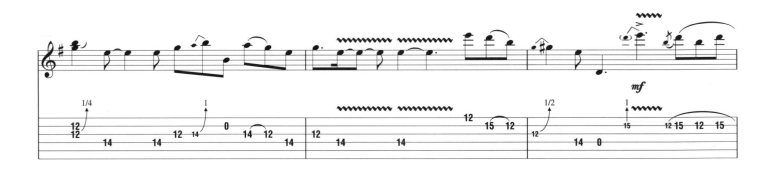

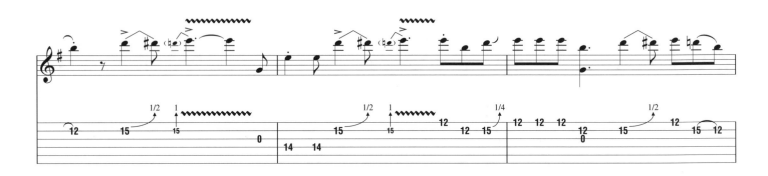

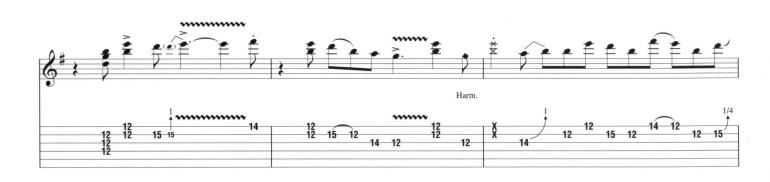

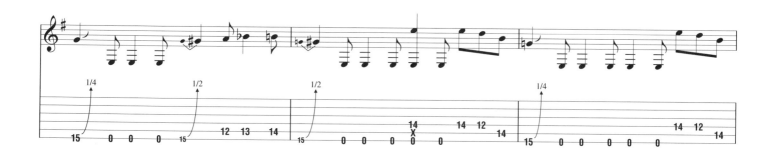

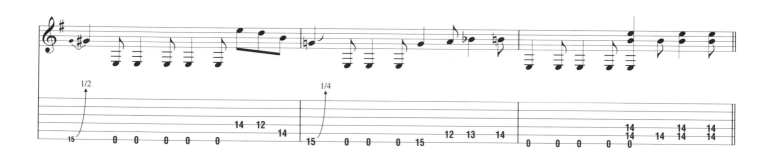

Verse

3. Way _____ o - ver yon - der ___ there's a moth - er, ___

way ___ in - side ___ of ___ her ___ stands a

sweet talk won't e - ven cause me pain.

Yeah, hey, ___ ma - chine ___ gun, ___ tear - in' all ___

___ a - round. ___

Outro

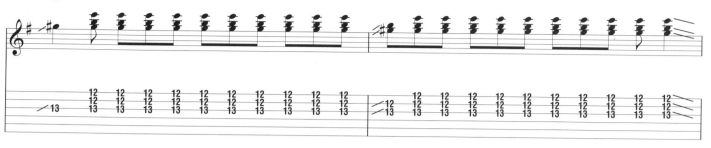

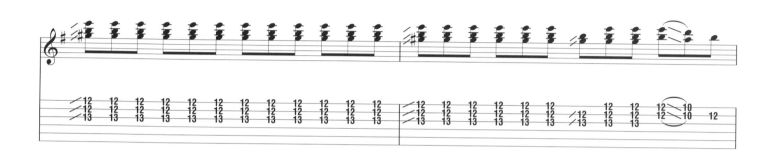

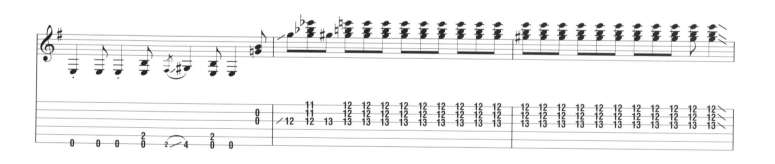

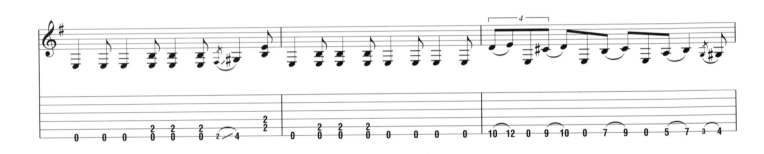

E

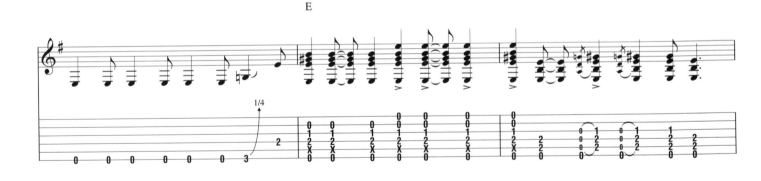

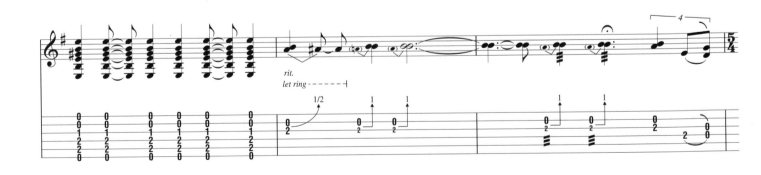

Free Time

E7

Yeah, yeah,_____ ma - chine gun! _____

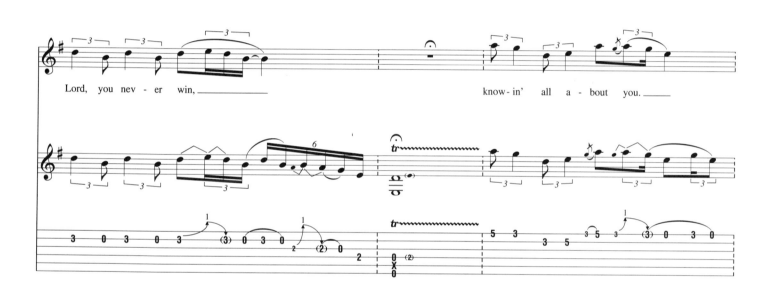

Lord, you nev - er win, _____   know - in' all a - bout you. _____

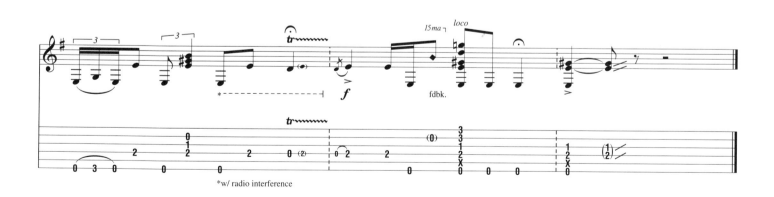

*w/ radio interference

Lover Man

Words and Music by Jimi Hendrix

*"Listen, it's gonna take, uh, time, uh, to like, get into it, because we're having little difficulties here and there...
but, like, if you can hold on a little bit I think we can all get it together, alright? [applause]
'Cause I'm gonna stay here all night until somebody moves." [more applause and cheering]*

Tune down 1/2 step:
(low to high) E♭-A♭-D♭-G♭-B♭-E♭

Intro

Moderate Rock ♩ = 144

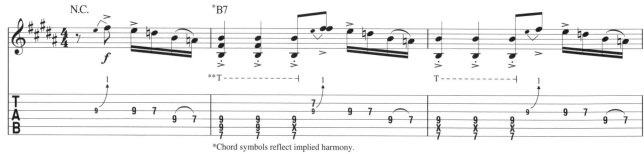

*Chord symbols reflect implied harmony.

**T = Thumb on 6th string

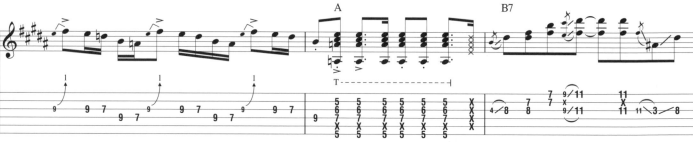

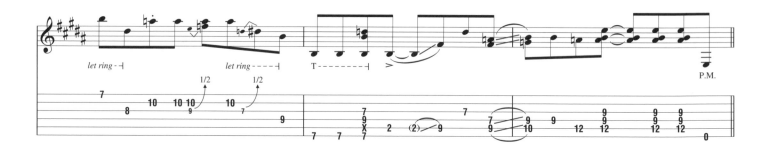

Verse

1. Here he comes, _ babe, here comes your lov - er man. _____

Uh, reach up, ba-by, hand me down my walk-

in' shoes.

I thought I'd run out of here, _____

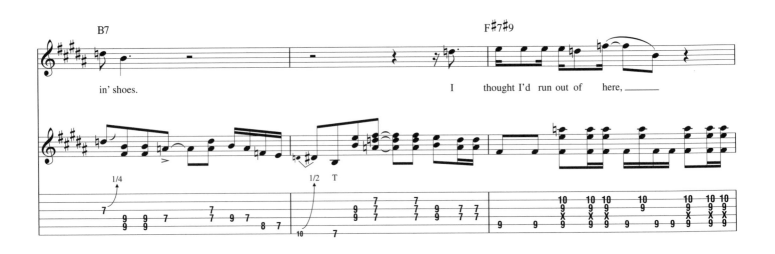

bet-ter off _ way down in San Soo. _____

Interlude

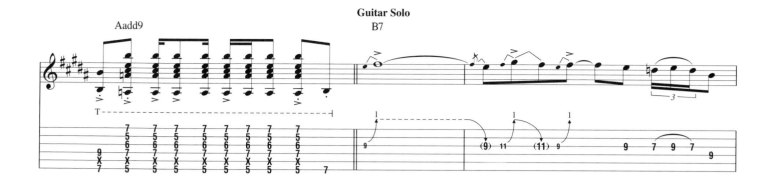

Guitar Solo

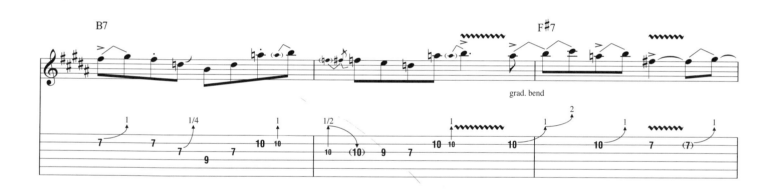

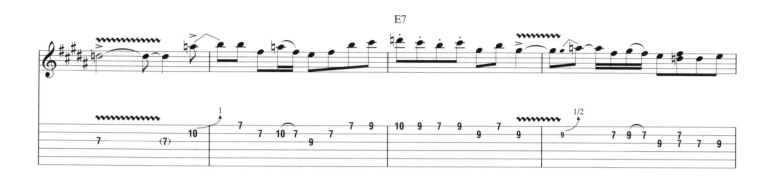

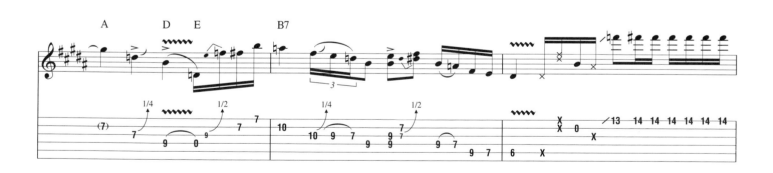

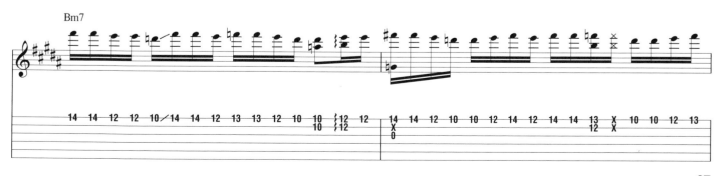

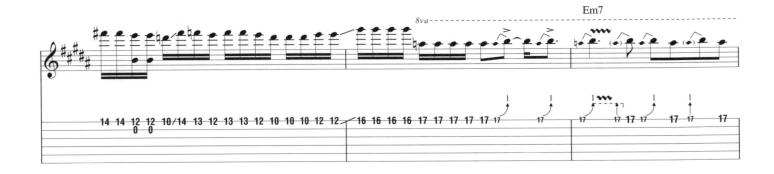

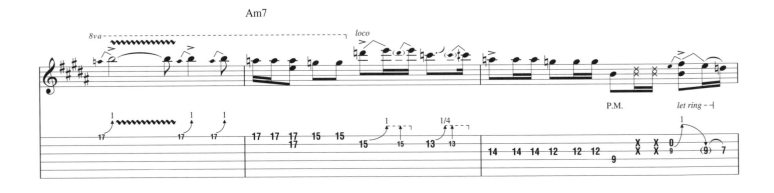

Interlude

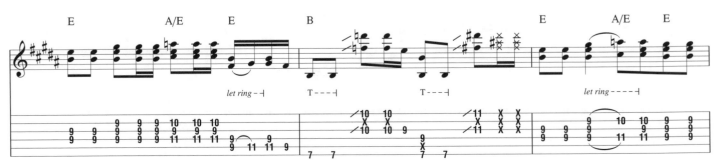

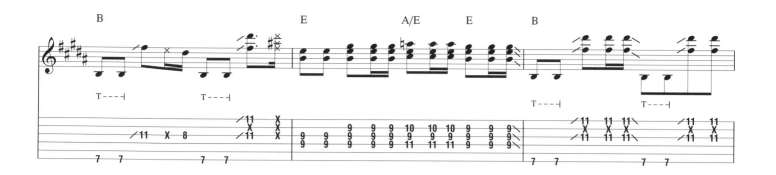

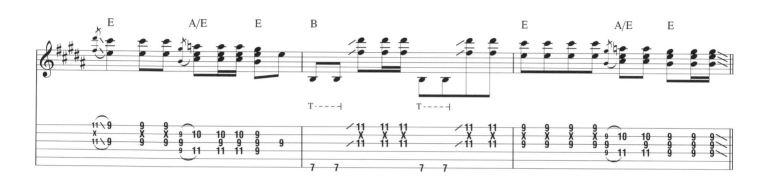

Outro

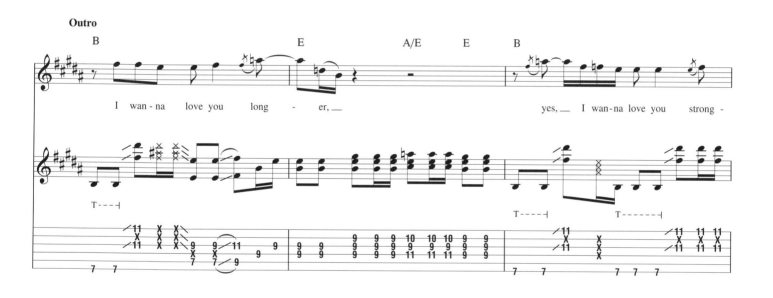

I wan-na love you long - er, ___ yes, ___ I wan-na love you strong -

er, ba - by. I wan-na love you long - er, all ___ you all.

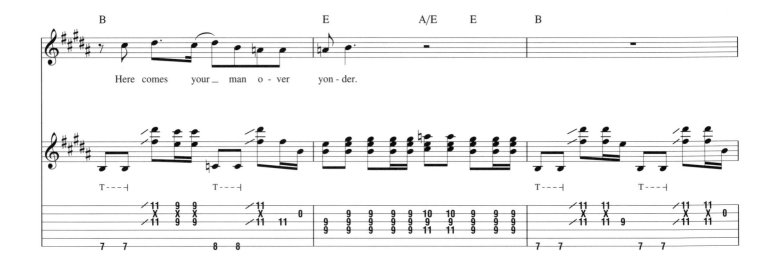

Here comes your _ man o - ver yon - der.

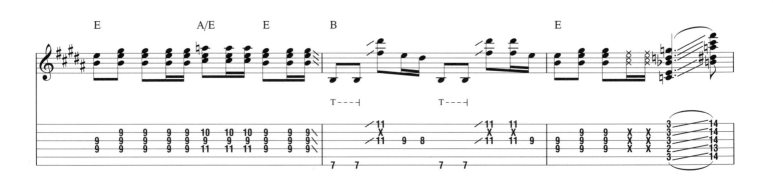

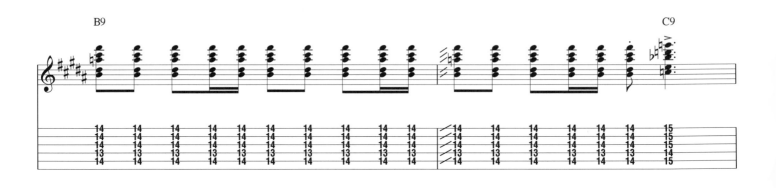

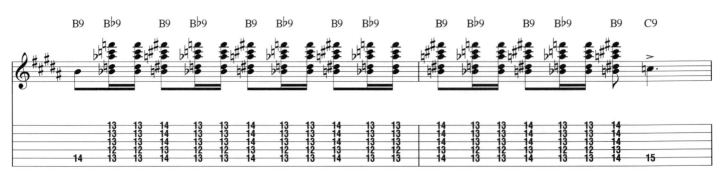

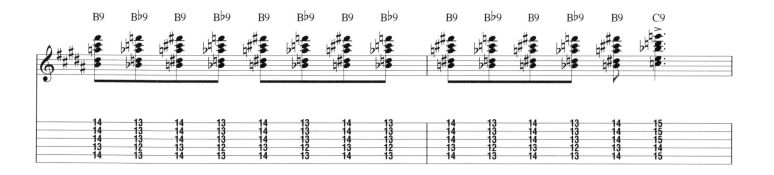

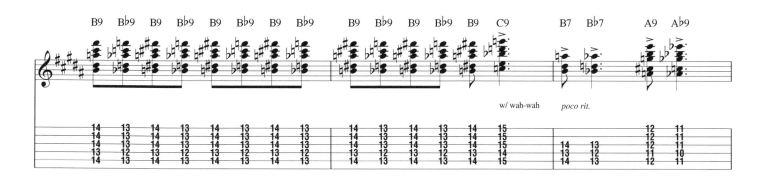

w/ wah-wah   *poco rit.*

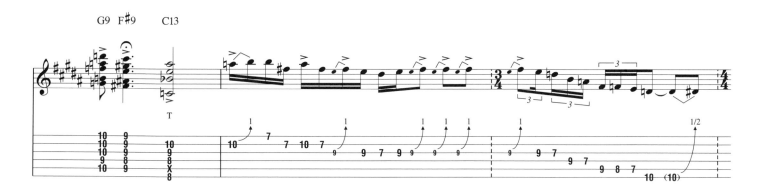

Pitch: G#   *Decrease volume w/ vol. knob.

Freedom
Words and Music by Jimi Hendrix

"Okay, we're gonna start all over again. Hello, how you doin', England? Glad to see you. We're (gonna) do a thing called 'Freedom.'"

Tune down 1/2 step:
(low to high) Eb-Ab-Db-Gb-Bb-Eb

Intro
Moderate Rock ♩ = 112

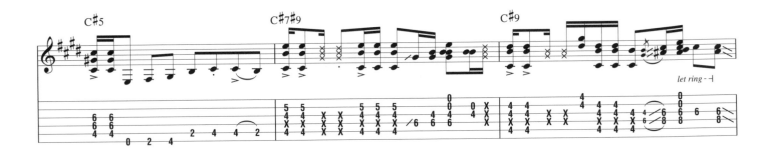

*Chord symbols reflect implied harmony.

Verse

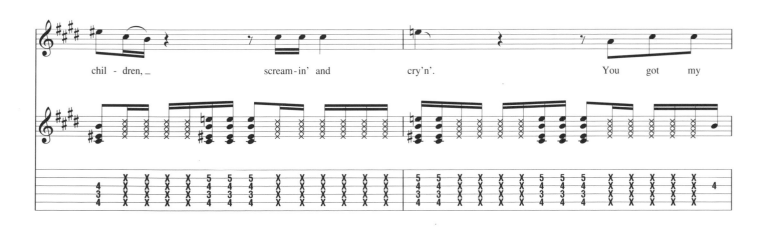

Chorus

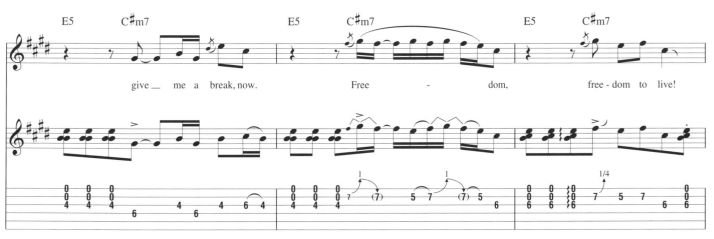

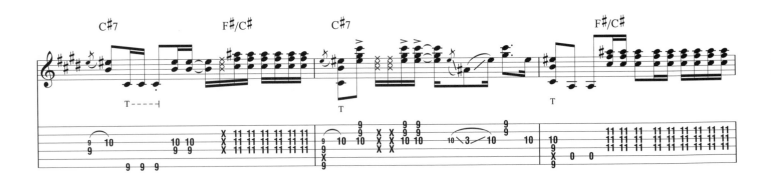

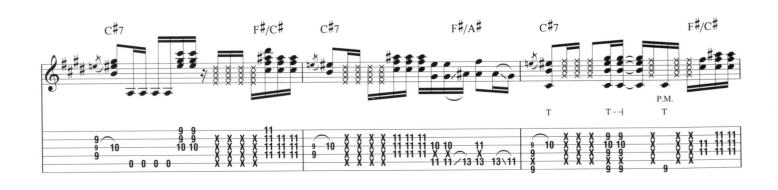

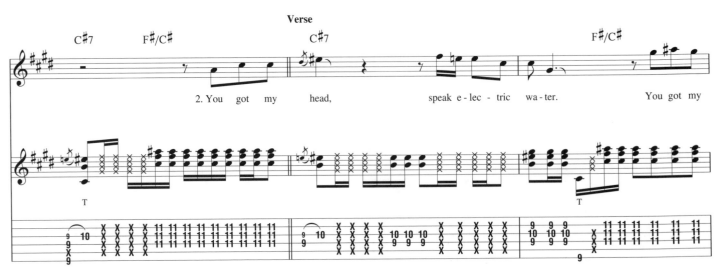

to ___ give now. ___ Free - dom, ___ got - ta live!

Free - dom, _ to you ___ I wan - na give.

Bridge

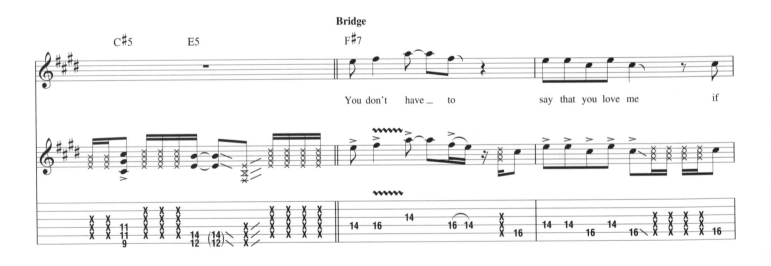

You don't have _ to say that you love me if

you don't mean _ (it,) you bet - ter be - lieve! If you need me or you

just wan-na bleed me, you bet-ter stick in your dag-ger some-one else. Set me free!

Guitar Solo

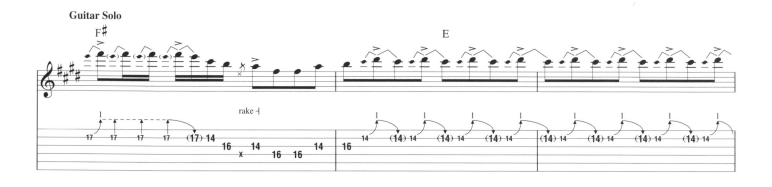

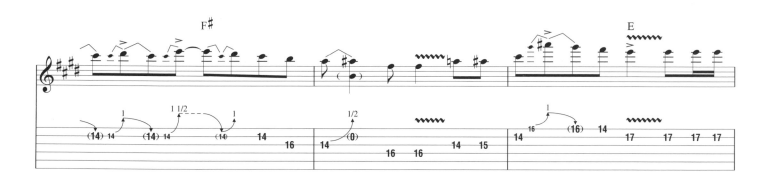

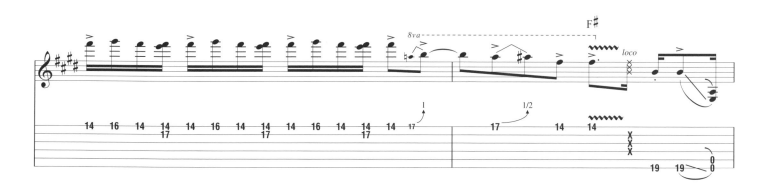

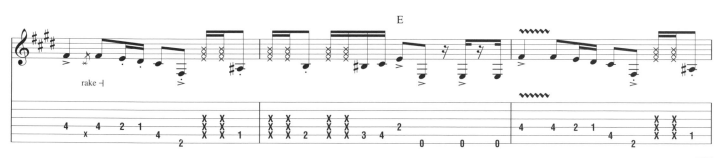

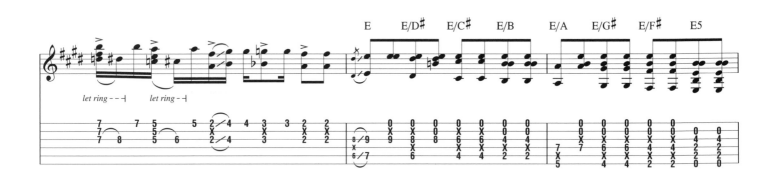

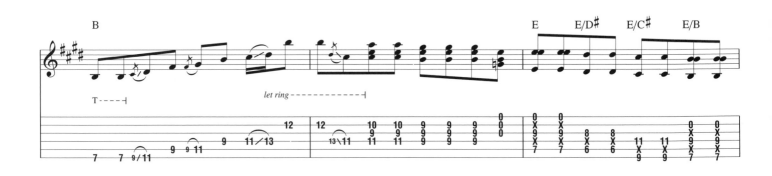

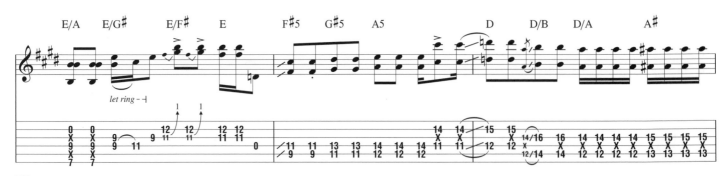

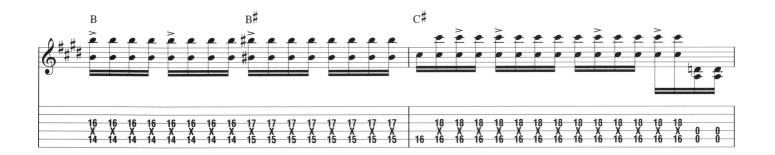

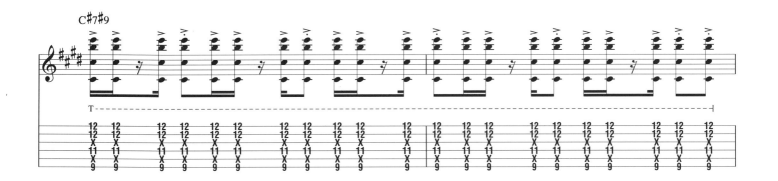

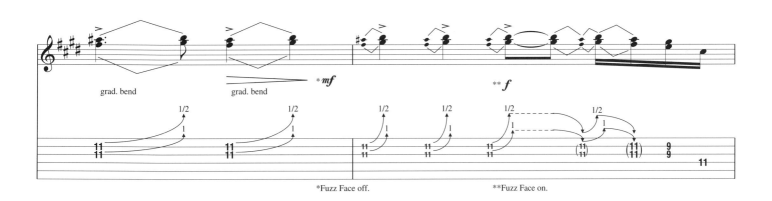

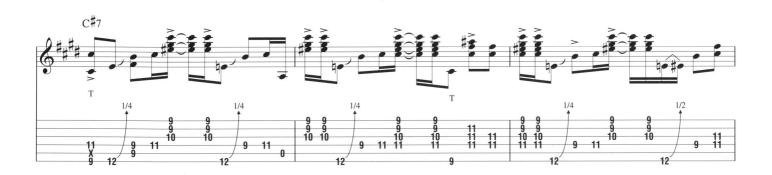

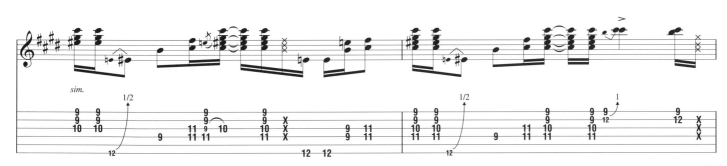

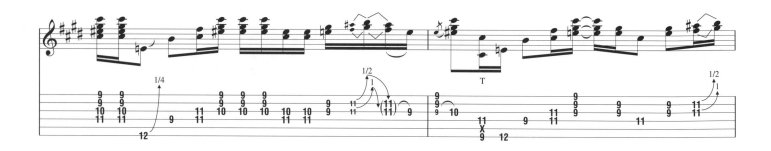

Chorus

C#m7

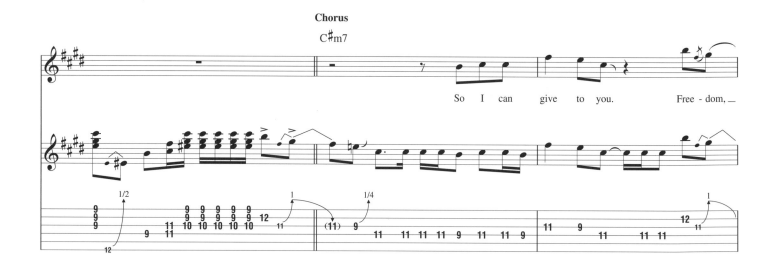

So I can give to you. Free - dom, ___

___ so you can have it, too. ___ Free - dom, _____ for my lit - tle chil -

- dren. ___ Free - dom, ___ you bet - ter...

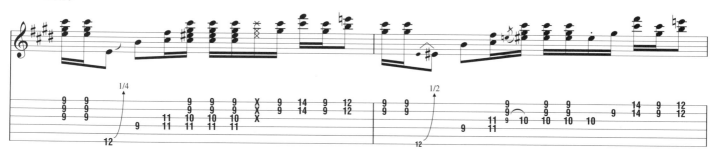

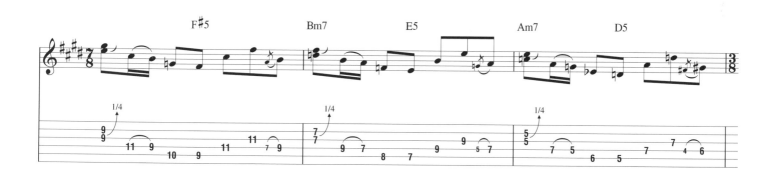

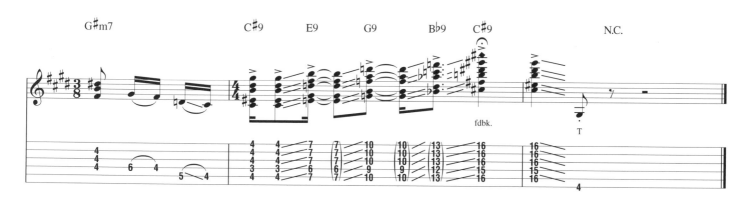

Red House

Words and Music by Jimi Hendrix

Tune down 1/2 step:
(low to high) Eb-Ab-Db-Gb-Bb-Eb

Intro
Slow Blues ♩. = 52

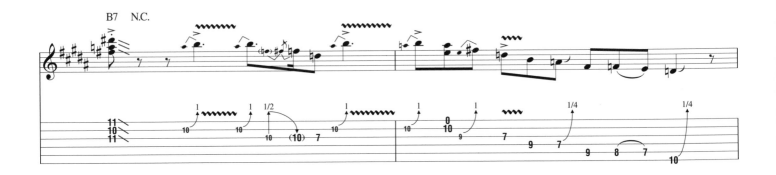

*Chord symbols reflect implied harmony.
**Begin with vol. knob positioned at 1/2 volume.

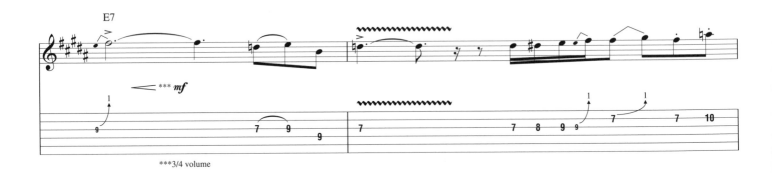

***3/4 volume

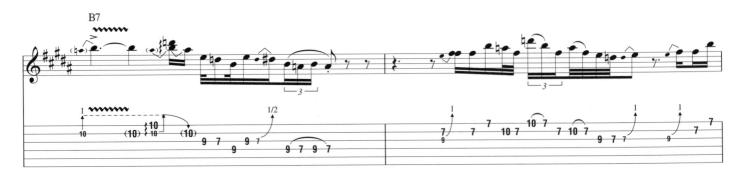

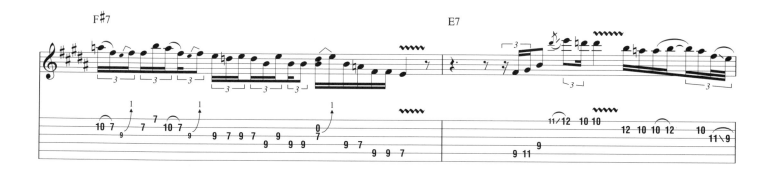

*Played behind the beat.

**T = Thumb on 6th string

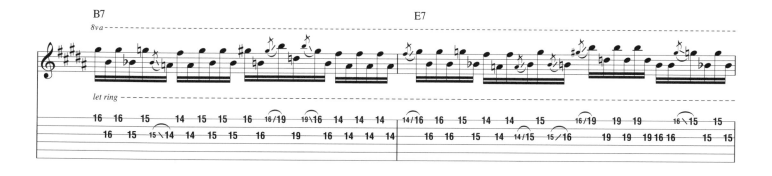

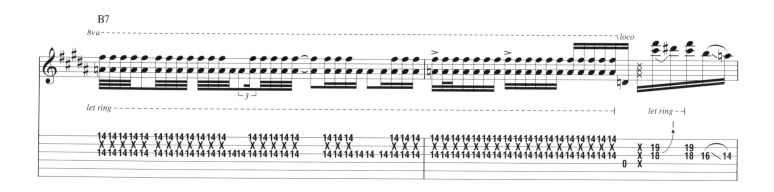

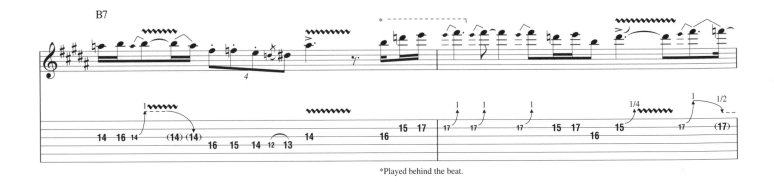

*Played behind the beat.

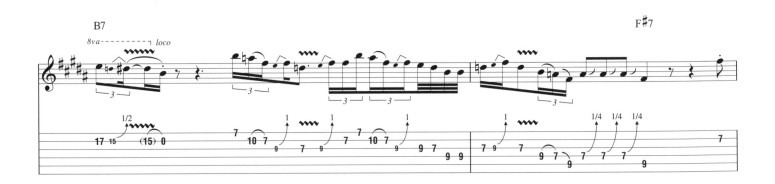

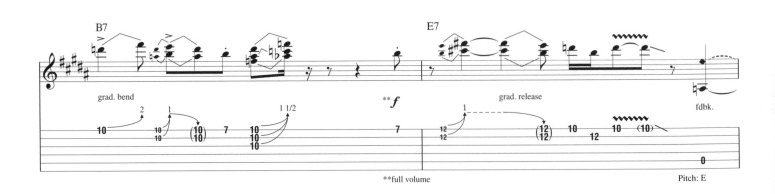

**full volume

Pitch: E

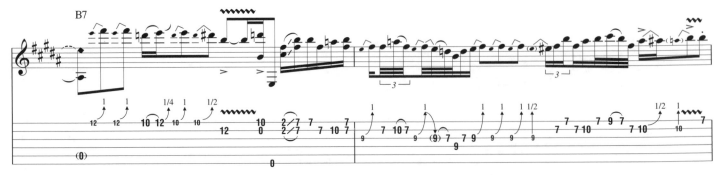

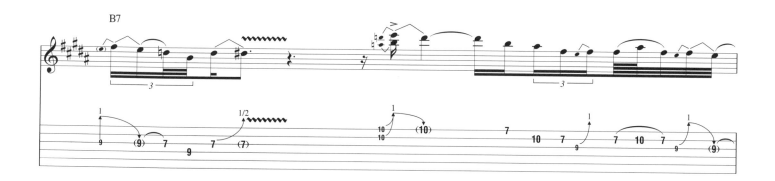

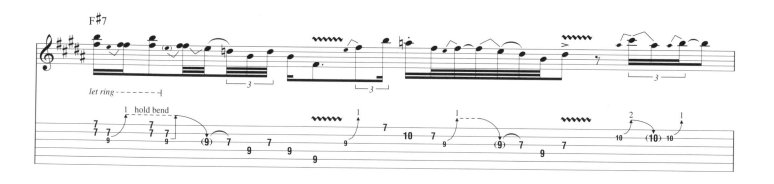

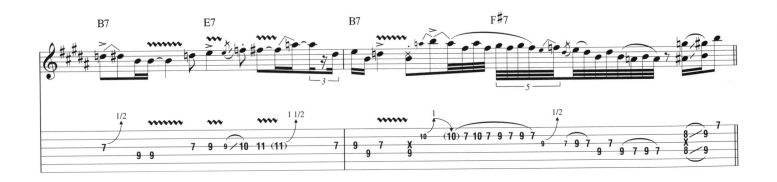

Verse

1. There's a red house o-ver yon - der, ba-by, thank God.

Lord, that's where my sweet ba - by

com-in' from.

Lord, there's a red house o-ver yon - der.

Lord, ____

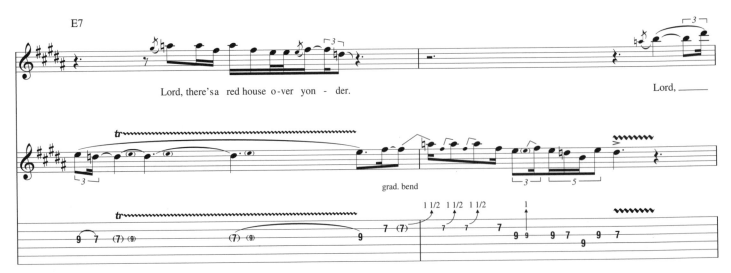

Lord have mer - cy, the key won't un - lock___ this door.___

*Played behind the beat.

Wait a min-ute, some-thing's wrong.___ We all know___ some-thing's wrong.___ Lord,

grad. bend

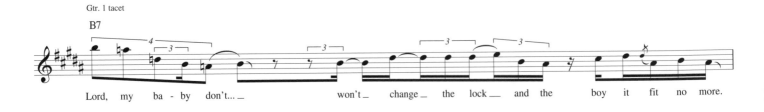

Gtr. 1 tacet

B7

Lord, my ba - by don't...___ won't___ change___ the lock___ and the boy it fit no more.

Spoken: Yeah, well, hell.

Gtr. 1

**f

**full volume

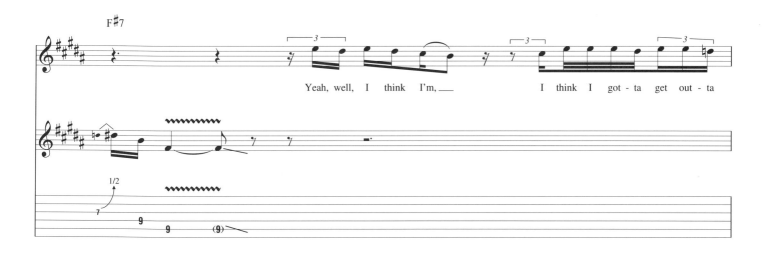

Yeah, well, I think I'm, ___ I think I got - ta get out - ta

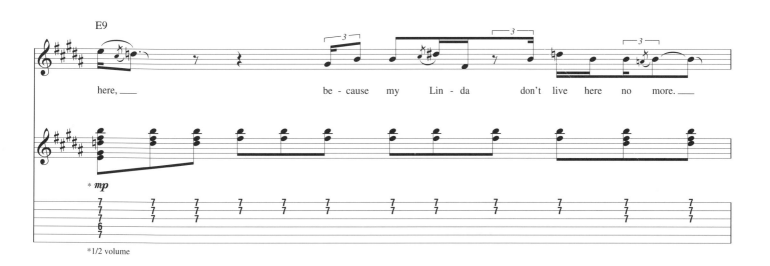

here, ___ be - cause my Lin - da don't live here no more. ___

*1/2 volume

**full volume

Guitar Solo

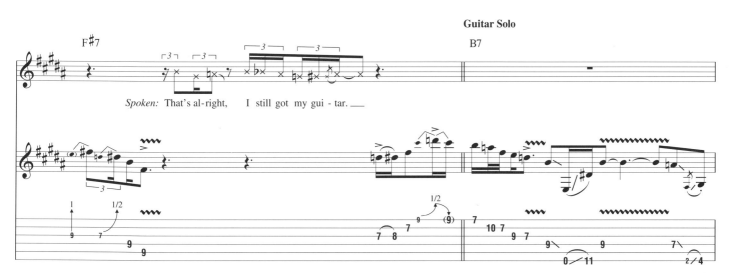

Spoken: That's al - right, I still got my gui - tar. ___

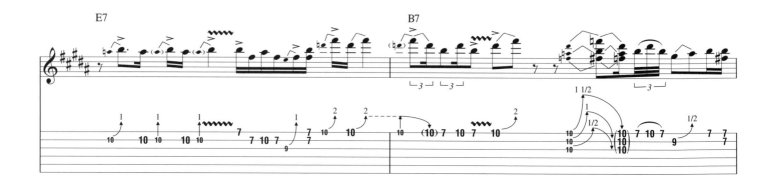

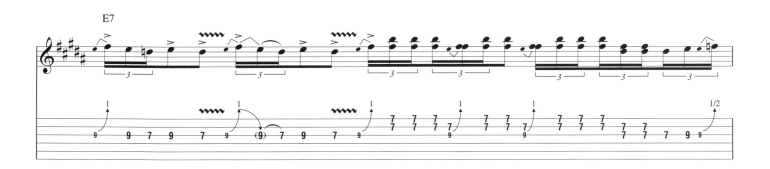

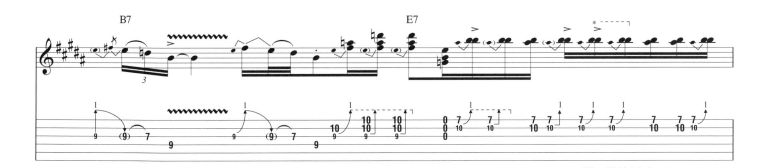

*Played behind the beat.

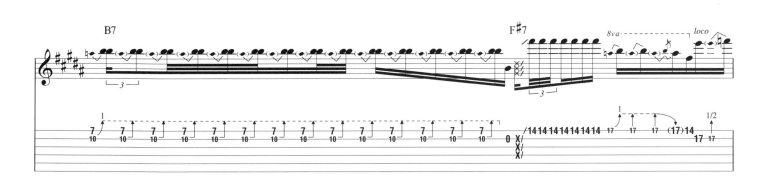

Double-time feel

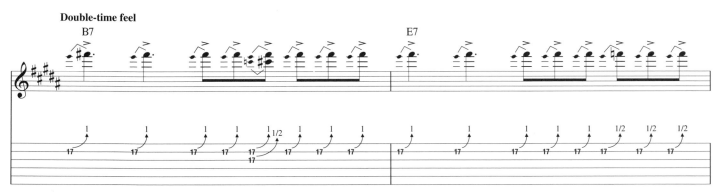

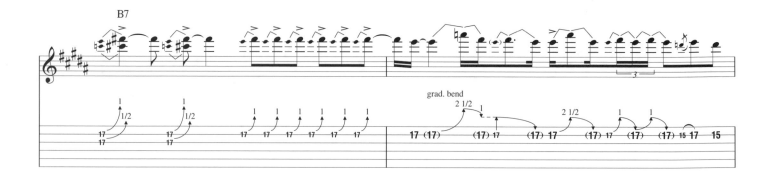

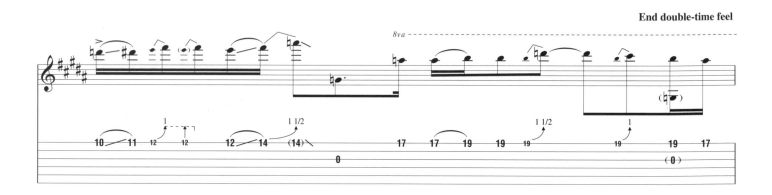

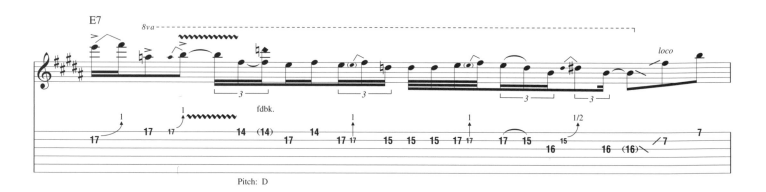

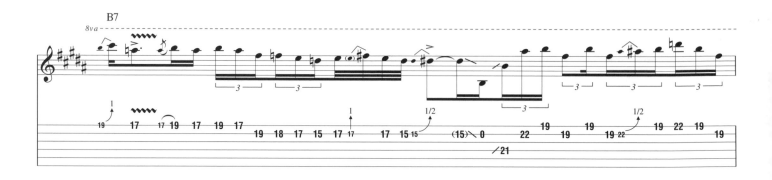

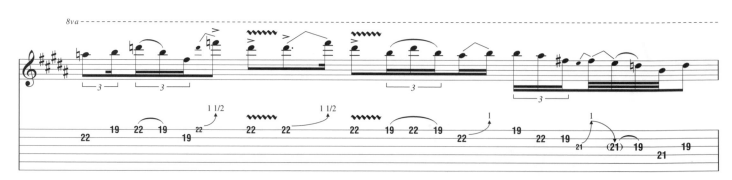

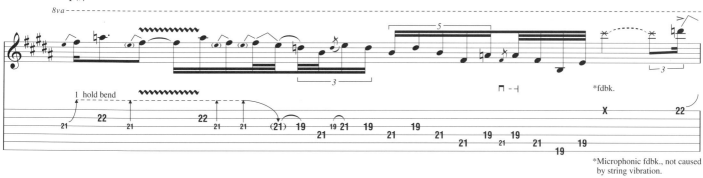

F#7

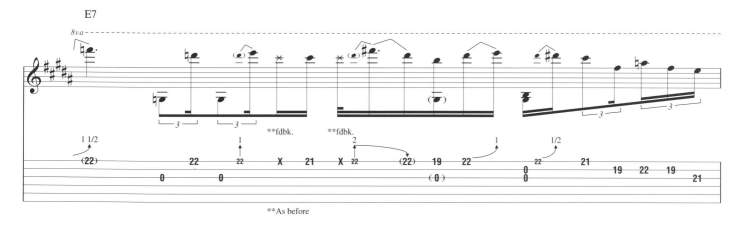

E7

*Microphonic fdbk., not caused
by string vibration.

**As before

B7

F#7

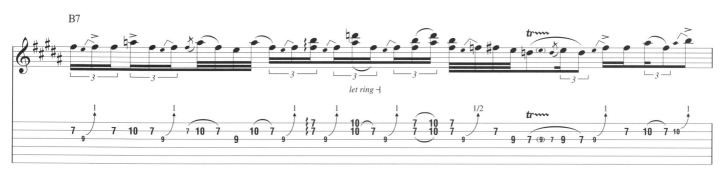

B7

*Played behind the beat.

*Played behind
the beat.

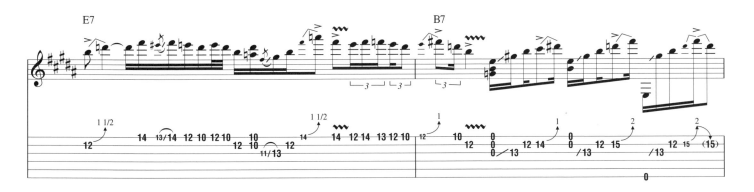

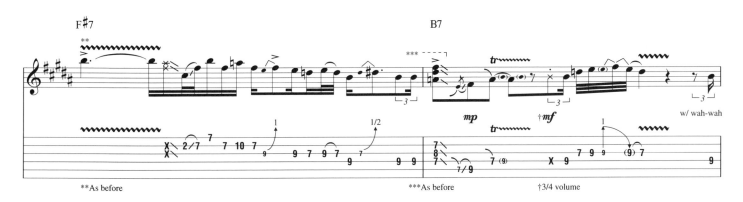

**As before   ***As before   †3/4 volume

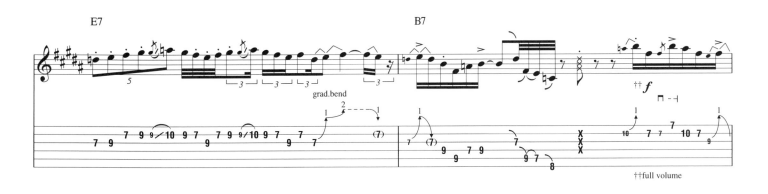

††full volume

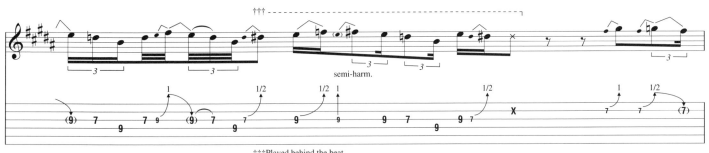

†††Played behind the beat.

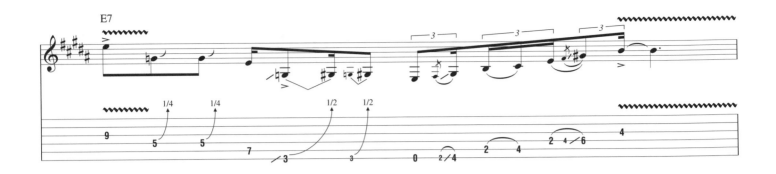

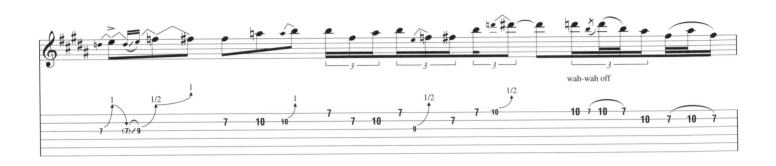

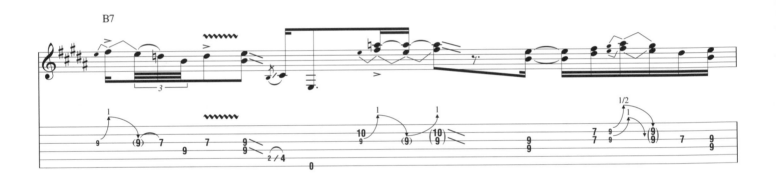

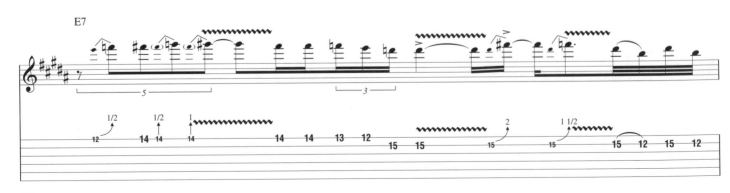

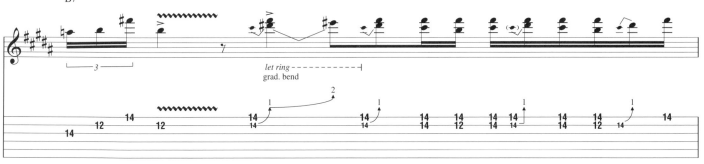

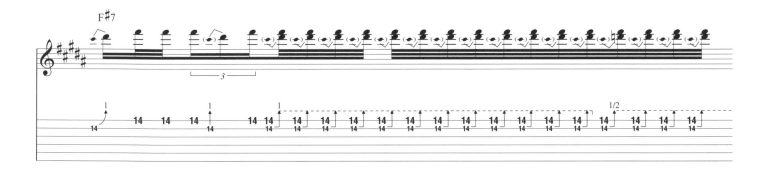

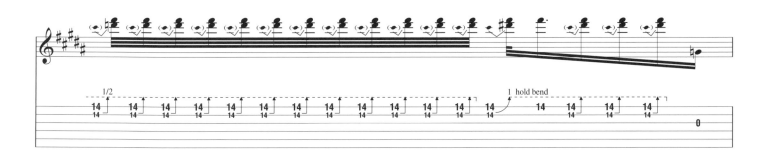

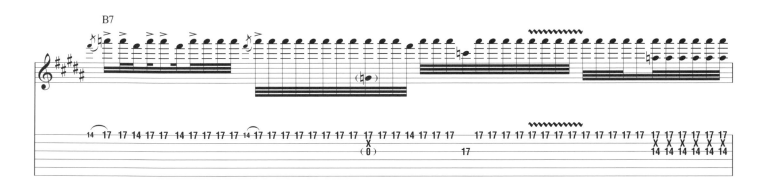

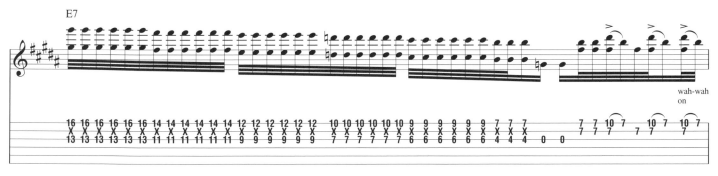

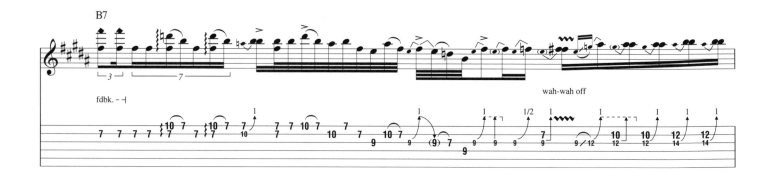

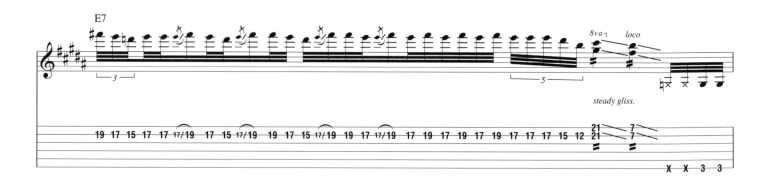

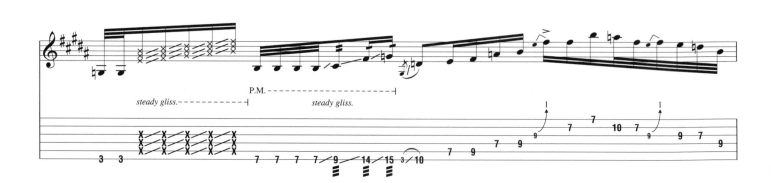

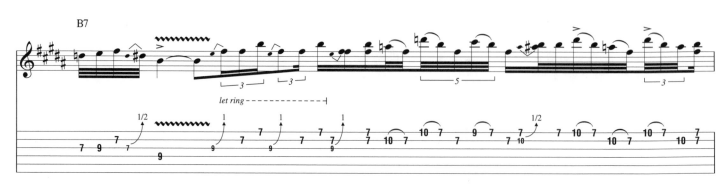

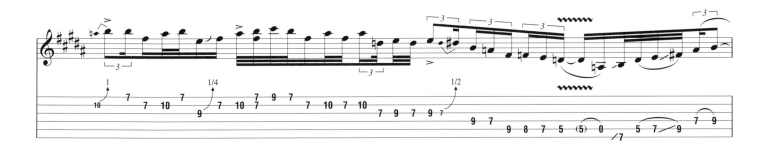

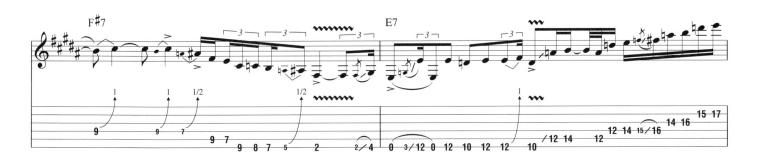

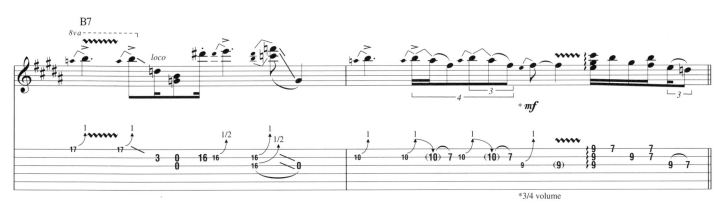

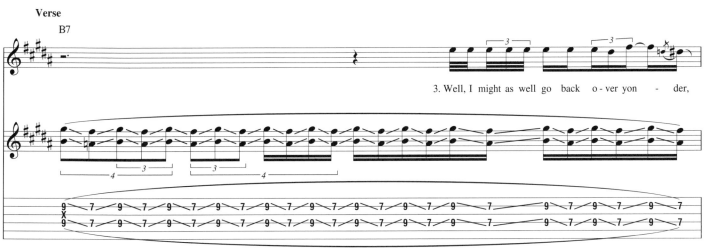

Verse

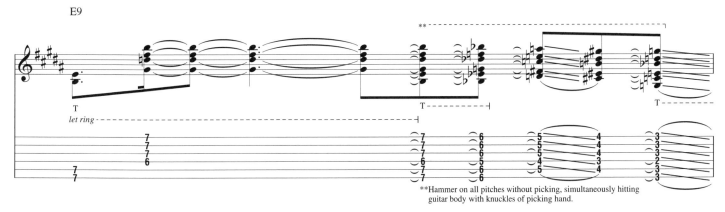

3. Well, I might as well go back o - ver yon - der,

**Hammer on all pitches without picking, simultaneously hitting
guitar body with knuckles of picking hand.

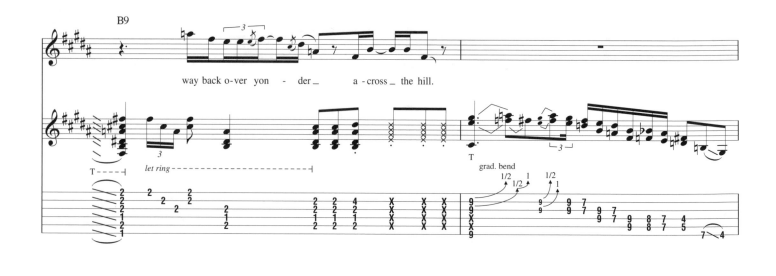

way back o-ver yon - der___ a-cross___ the hill.

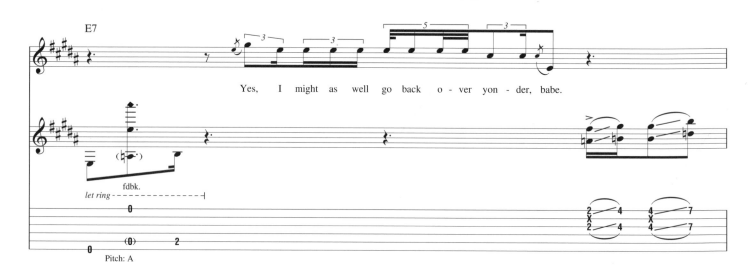

Yes, I might as well go back o - ver yon - der, babe.

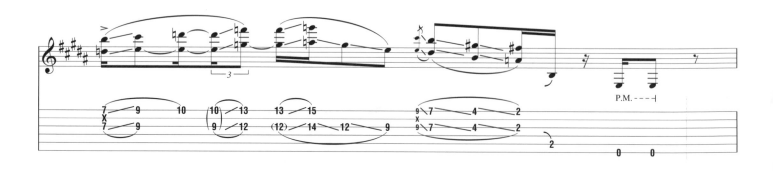

Lord, ___ way o - ver yon - der, 'cross the hill. ___

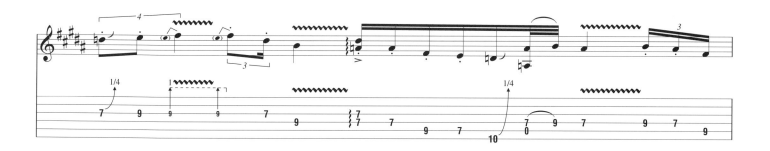

If my ba - by don't love ___ me no more, ___ like she say they don't,

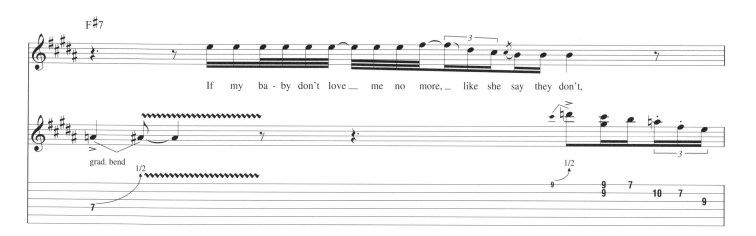

Lord, I know good and well ___ that her sis - ter will! ___

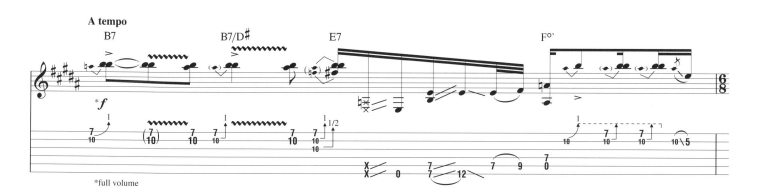

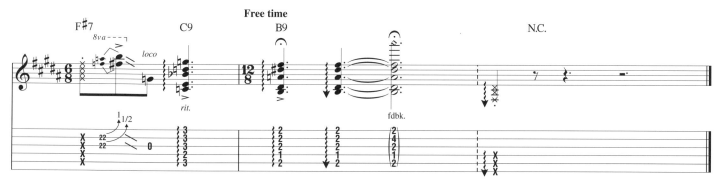

Dolly Dagger

Words and Music by Jimi Hendrix

*"Oh yeah, somebody wants the people in the front row to sit down. I think it's commoners from the hills.
Don't forget, you can't fly off the top of those hills, don't forget that."*

Tune down 1/2 step:
(low to high) Eb-Ab-Db-Gb-Bb-Eb

Intro

Moderate Rock ♩ = 126

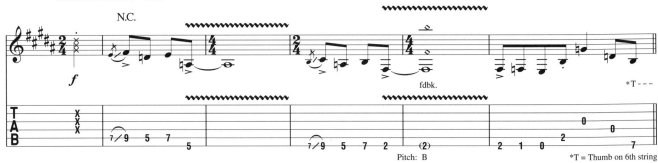

Chorus

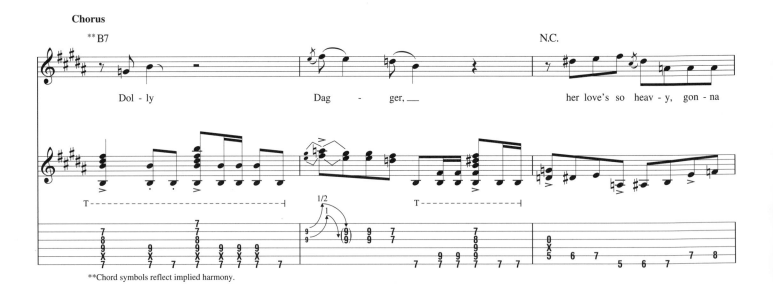

Dol - ly   Dag - ger, ___   her love's so heav - y, gon - na

**Chord symbols reflect implied harmony.

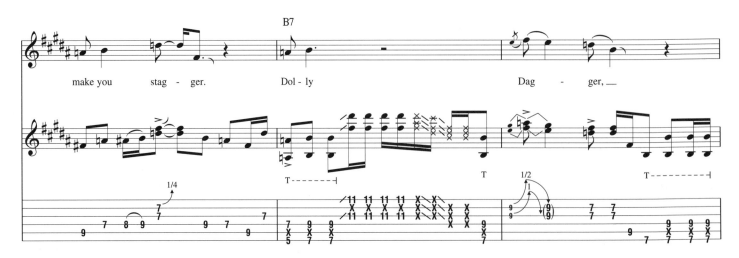

make you   stag - ger.   Dol - ly   Dag - ger, ___

she drinks the blood from the jag - ged edge. _

Interlude

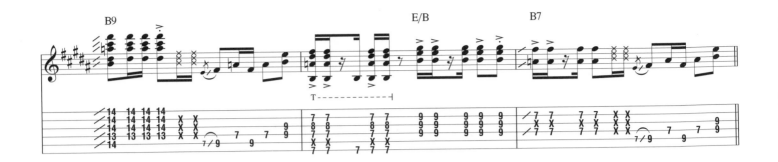

Chorus

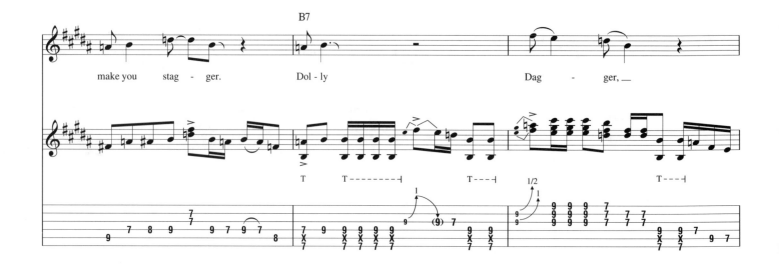

make you stag-ger. Dol-ly Dag - ger, ___

She ain't sat - is - fied 'til she gets what she's af - ter.

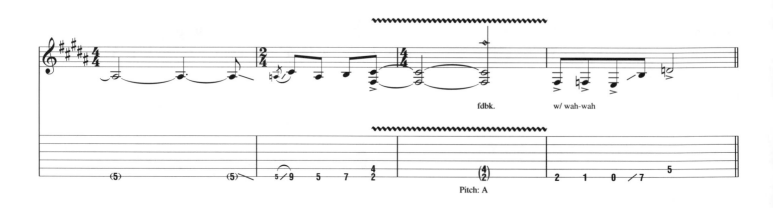

fdbk.   w/ wah-wah

Pitch: A

Guitar Solo

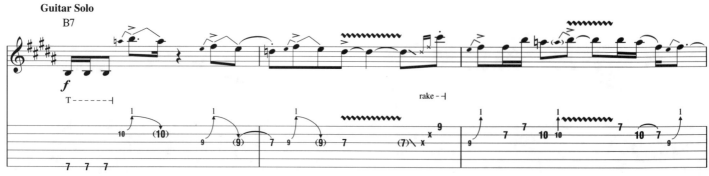

rake

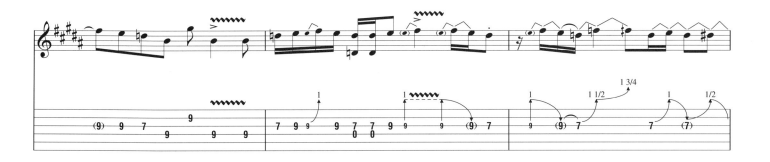

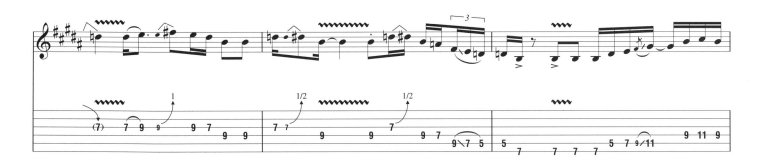

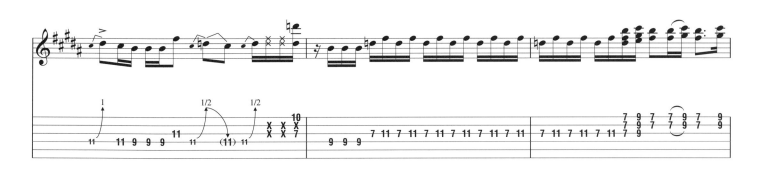

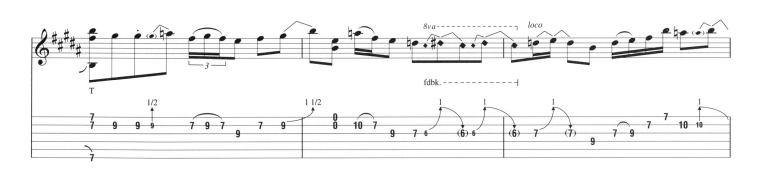

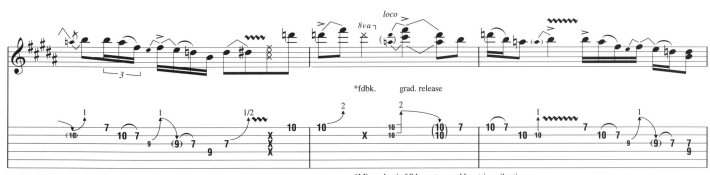

*fdbk.   grad. release

*Microphonic fdbk., not caused by string vibration.

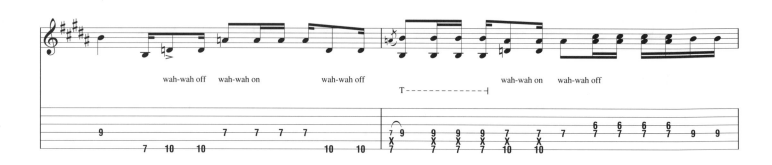

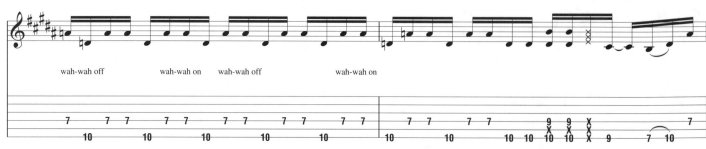

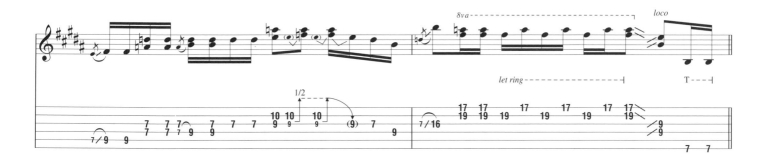

Interlude

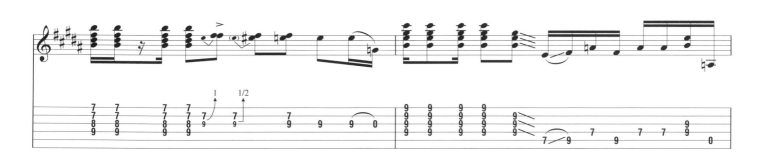

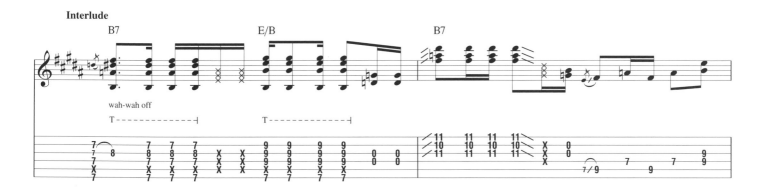

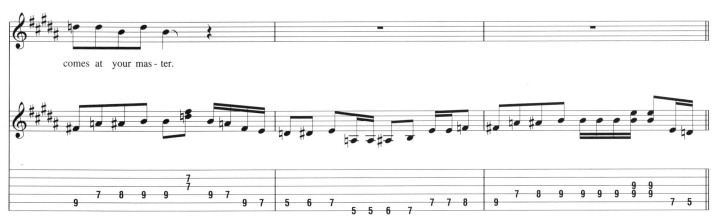

Interlude

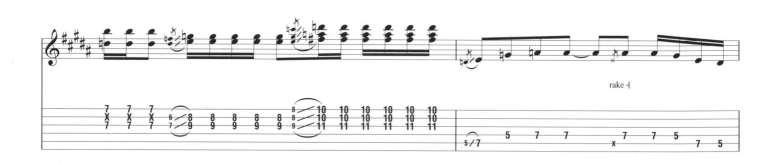

Outro-Guitar Solo

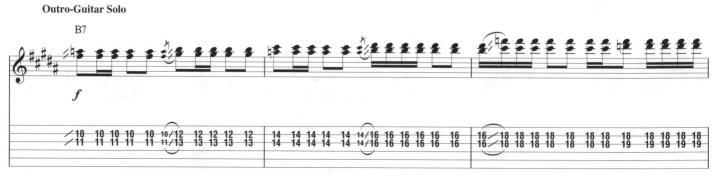

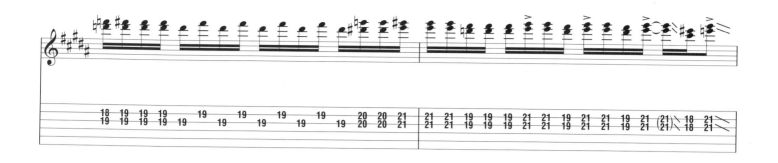

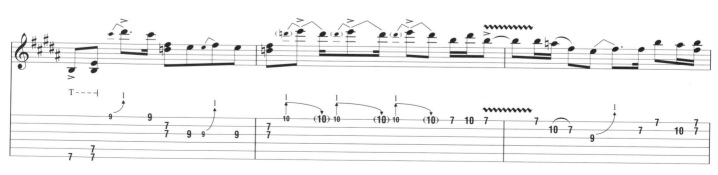

113

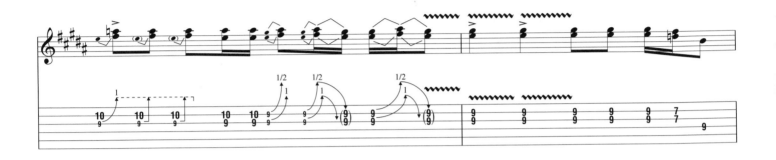

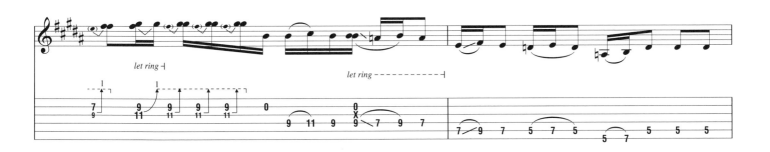

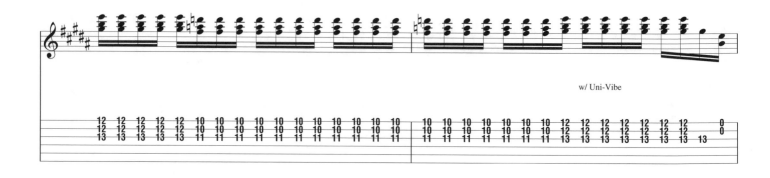

w/ Uni-Vibe

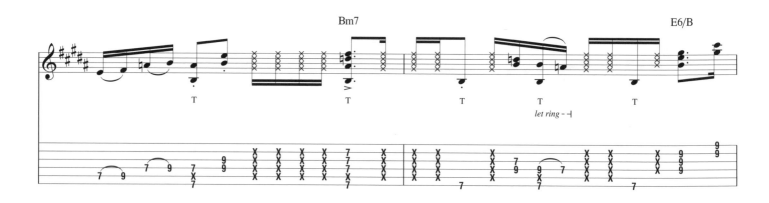

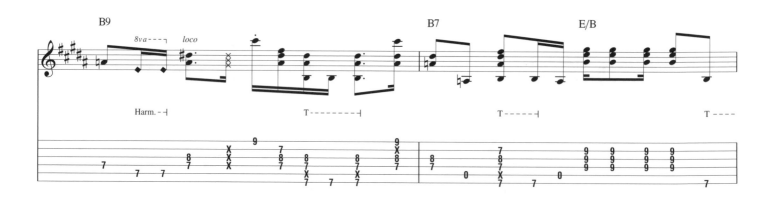

Free time

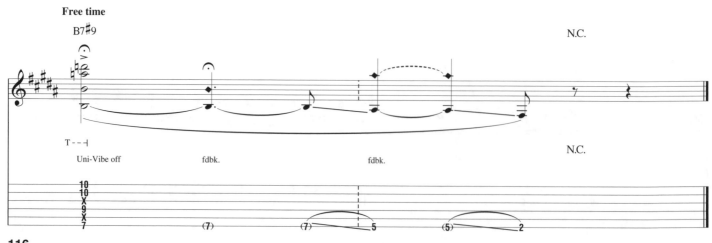

Midnight Lightning

Words and Music by Jimi Hendrix

"Very sorry for tuning up, but, uh, you know, we do that, uh, to protect your ears. That's why we don't play so loud, you know? And, uh, cowboys, you know, won't stay in tune anyway. I'm so glad you all have patience, though, 'cause I don't. I'm gonna do this slow blues."

Tune down 1/2 step:
(low to high) E♭-A♭-D♭-G♭-B♭-E♭

Intro
Moderately slow ♩ = 69

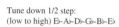

*Chord symbols reflect basic harmony.

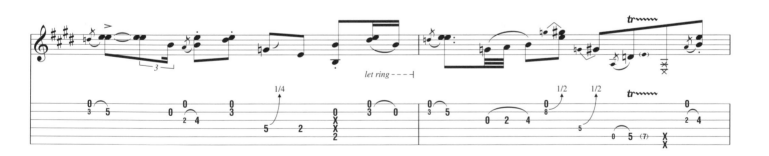

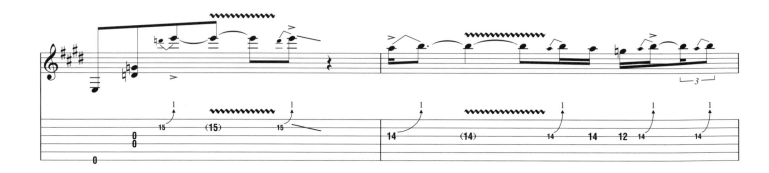

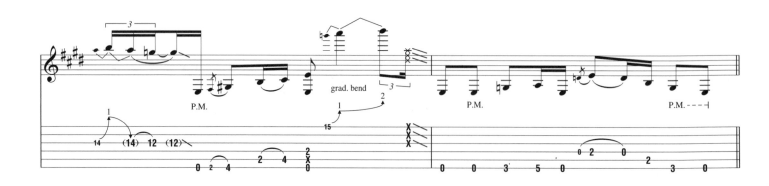

Verse

E7

1. We got - ta keep mov - in',   got - ta keep on groov - in',

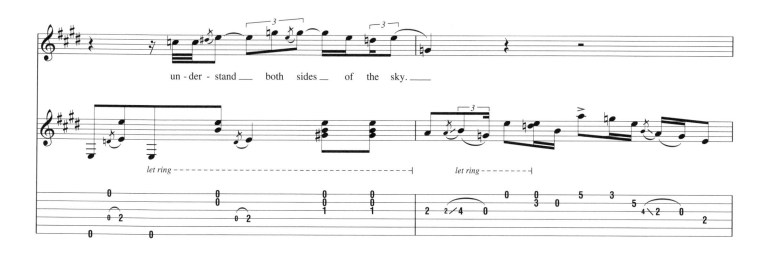

un - der - stand __ both sides __ of the sky. __

You got - ta keep on ___ lov - in',   good, sweet lov - in',

make love   on my   dy - in' bed.

Interlude

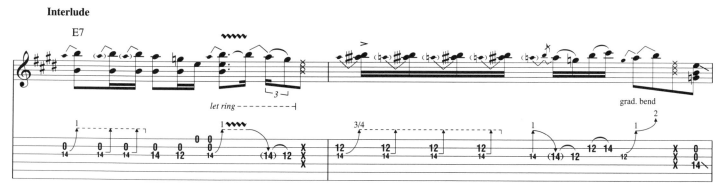

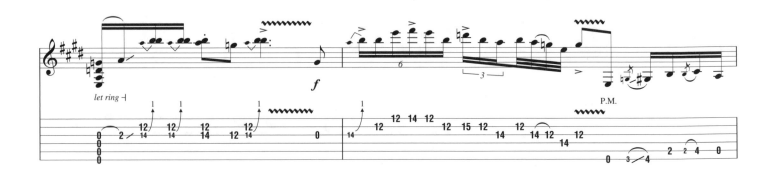

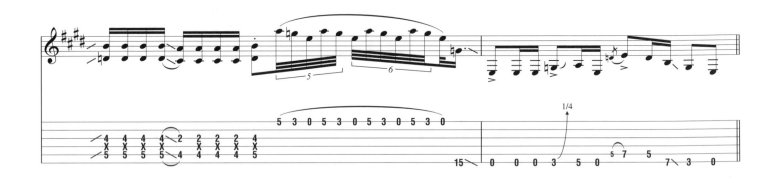

Verse

E7

2. I get stoned, but I can't call home, _ but I'm call-in' long dis-tance on a

don't look back. _____   Mid - night light - nin' strik - in' right now.

Got - ta keep on lov - in',

I mean good, sweet lov - in'.   Make love on my dy - in' bed.

Love! _____

Guitar Solo

E7

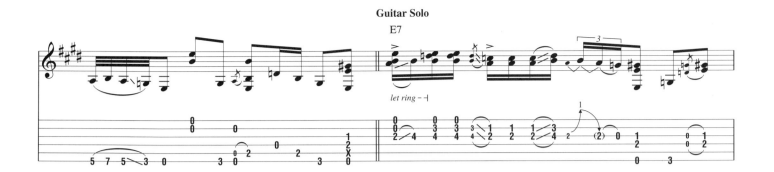

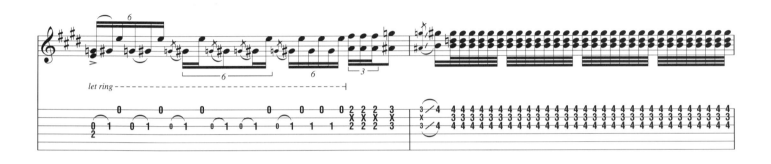

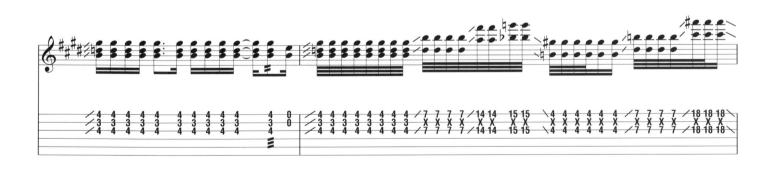

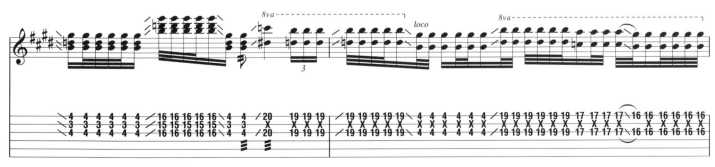

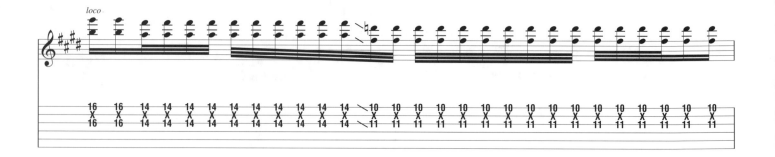

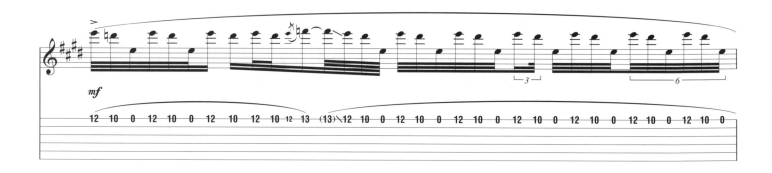

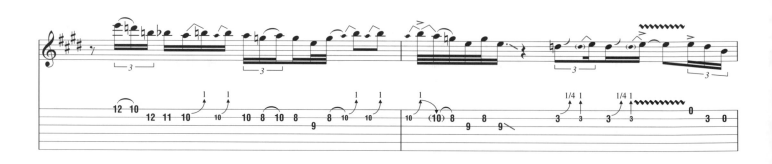

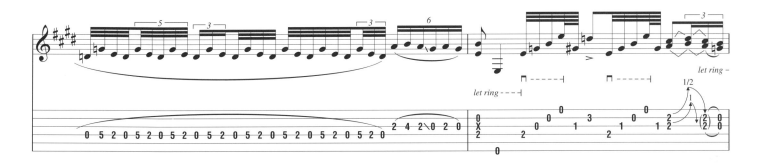

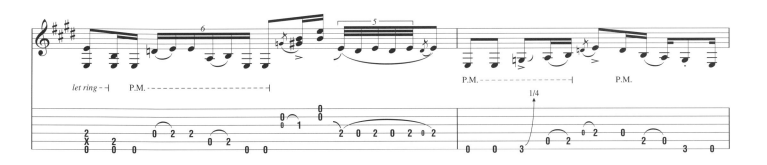

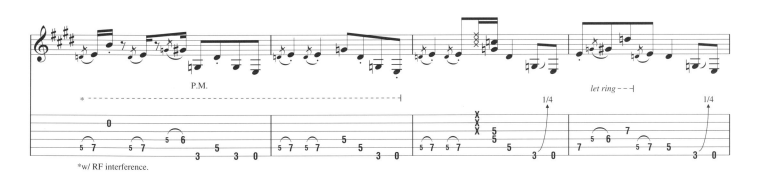

*w/ RF interference.

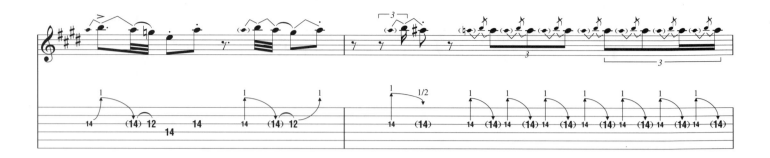

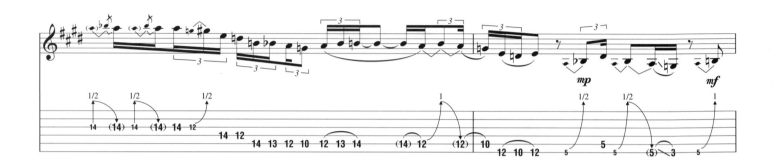

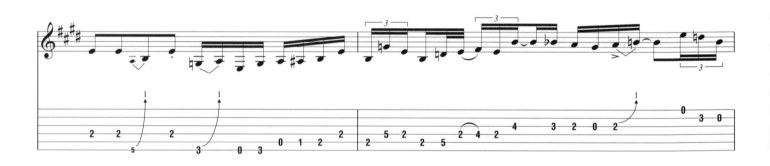

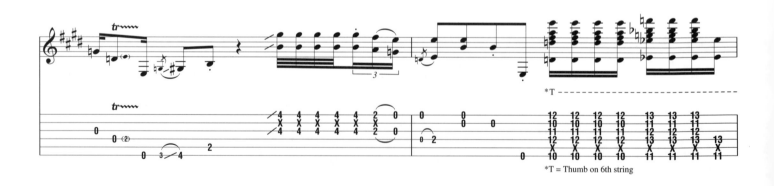

*T = Thumb on 6th string

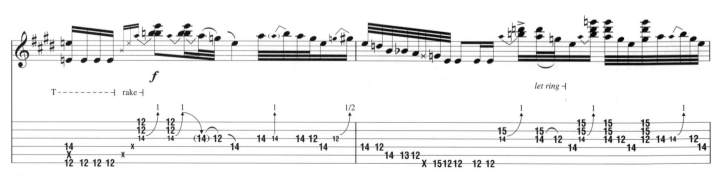

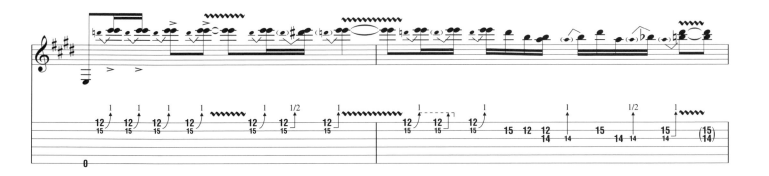

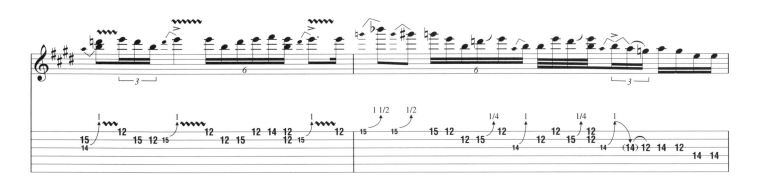

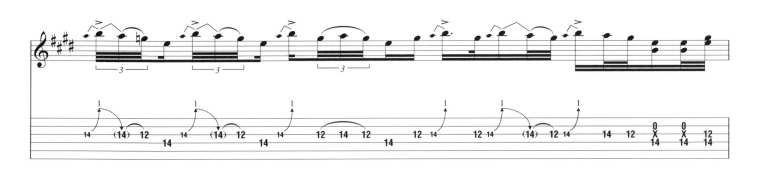

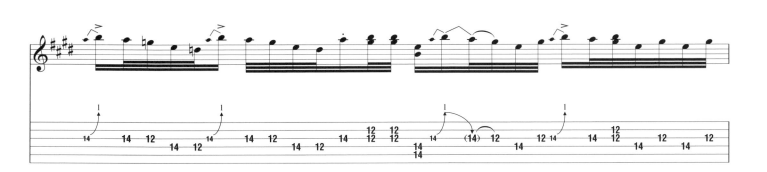

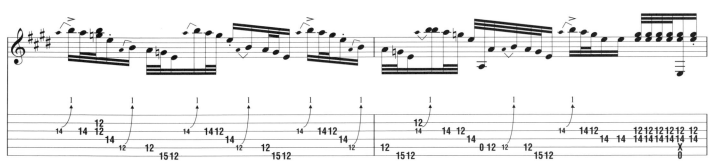

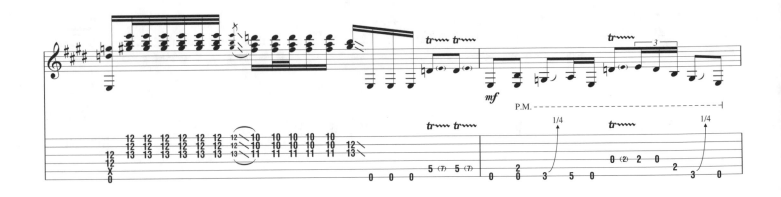

Begin fade

Fade out

Foxey Lady

Words and Music by Jimi Hendrix

"This is dedicated to Linda, to the cat right there with the silver face, dedicated to Kirsten, Karen, and, uh, the little four-year-old girl over there with the yellow jeans. And I'd like to say thank you for the last three years...one of these days we'll get together again. Thanks for showing up, you're outta sight! If you want the same old songs, we can do that."

Tune down 1/2 step:
(low to high) E♭-A♭-D♭-G♭-B♭-E♭

Intro
Free time

Moderate Rock ♩ = 108

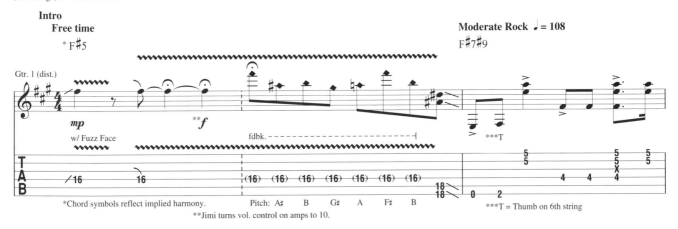

*Chord symbols reflect implied harmony.
**Jimi turns vol. control on amps to 10.
***T = Thumb on 6th string

Pitch: A♯ B G♯ A F♯ B

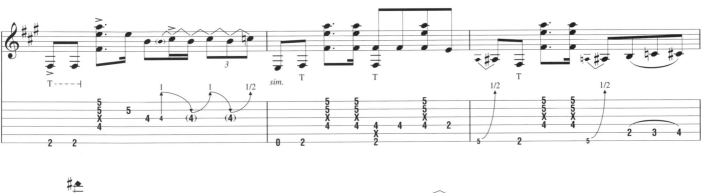

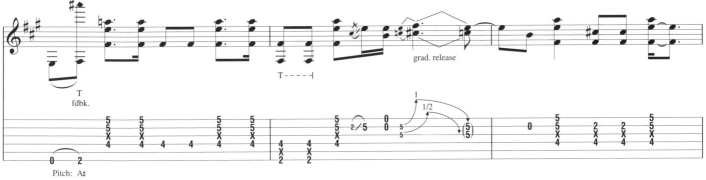

Pitch: A♯

Verse

F♯7♯9

1. Uh, you know   you're a sweet lit-tle heart-break-er,

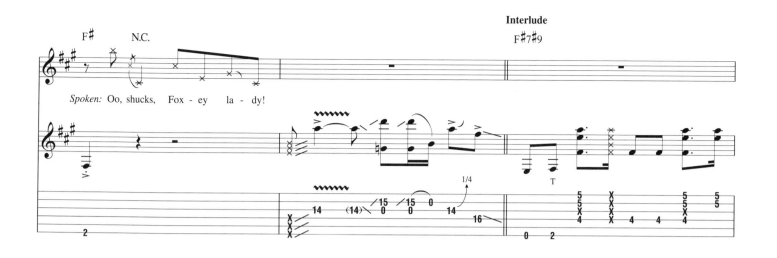

Spoken: Oo, shucks, Fox - ey la - dy!

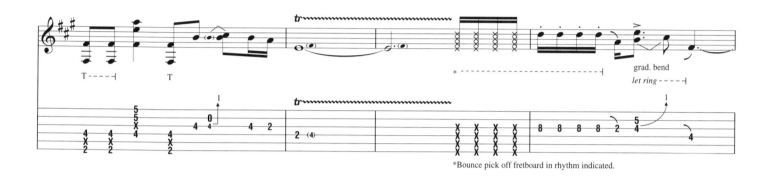

*Bounce pick off fretboard in rhythm indicated.

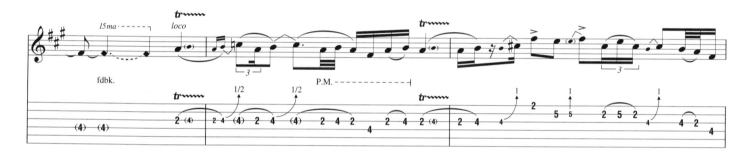

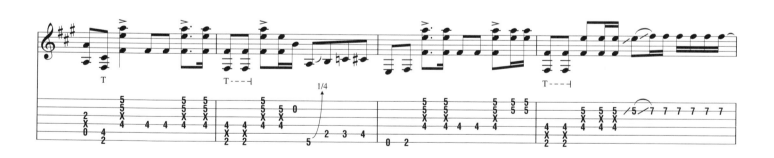

**Jimi goes behind his amps to fix his pants, resulting in
extraneous noise from effects pedals (next 9 1/2 meas.).

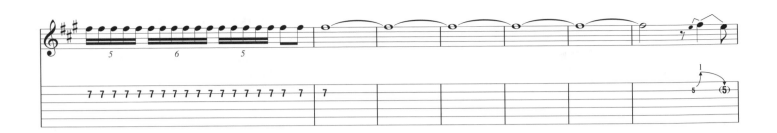

*Jimi re-emerges from behind his amps.

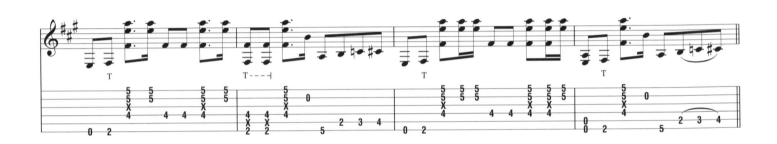

Verse

F#7#9

2. Now, I   see you   all   down on the scene, ba - by.   *Spoken:* Oh, Fox - ey...

You make me   wan-na   get up and scream!

Guitar Solo

F#7#9

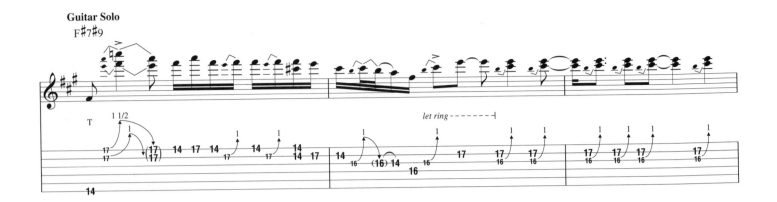

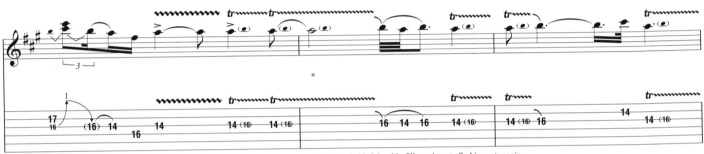

*Jimi goes behind the side-fill monitors to fix his pants again.

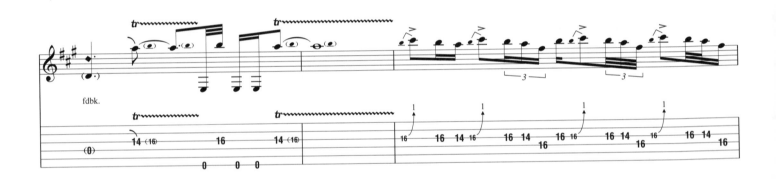

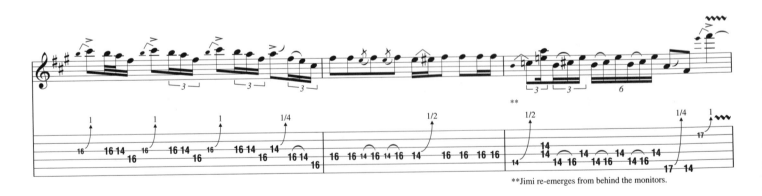

**Jimi re-emerges from behind the monitors.

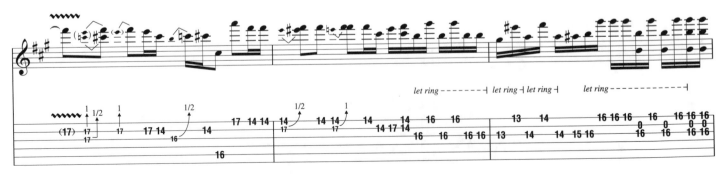

134

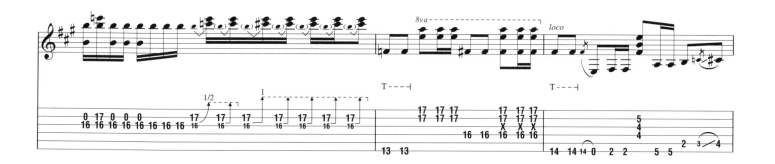

Interlude

F#5

Gtr. 1 tacet
(Bass & Drums)

29

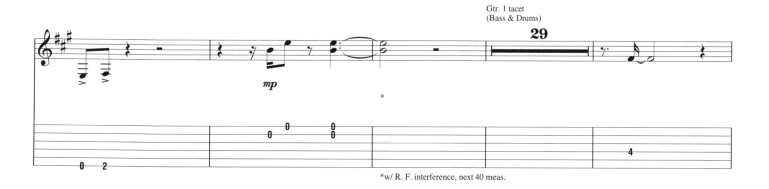

*w/ R. F. interference, next 40 meas.

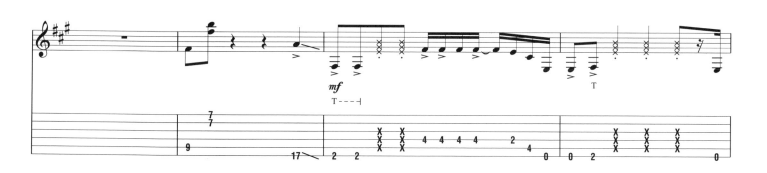

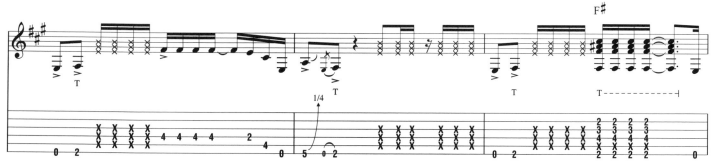

F#7#9

*Harm. located
four-tenths the
distance
between 2nd
& 3rd frets.

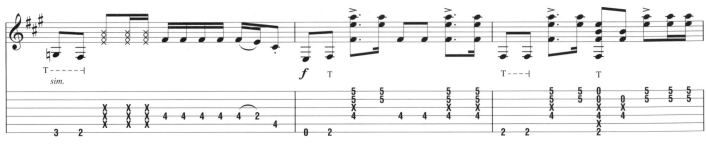

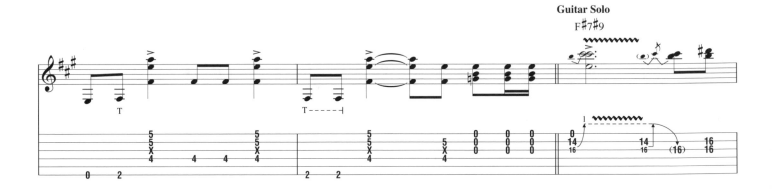

Guitar Solo

F#7#9

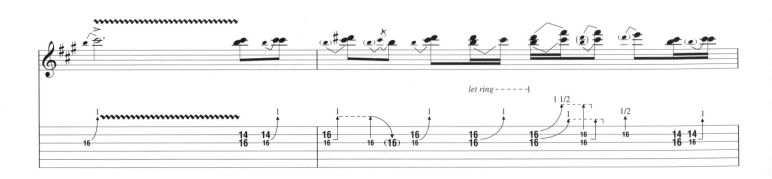

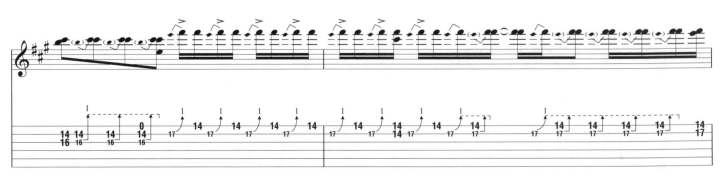

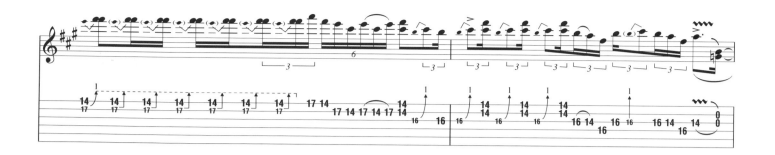

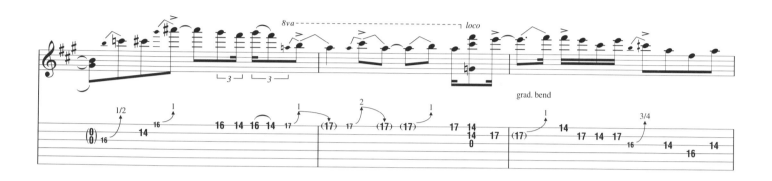

*Jimi tunes up his guitar.

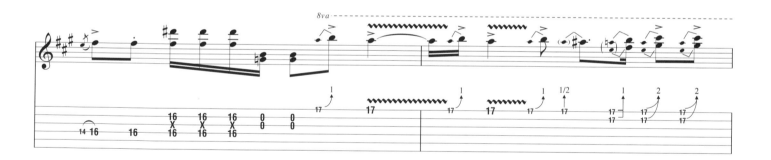

Chorus

F#7#9

I ain't gon-na do you harm.

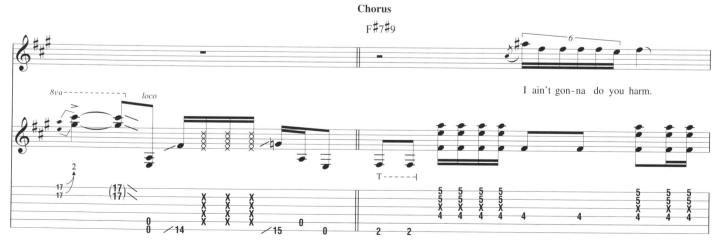

I won't do you no harm.

You got to be all mine.

Spoken: Oo, Fox - ey, the next time, uh...

Outro

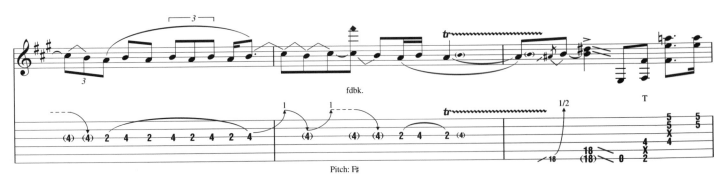

Pitch: F#

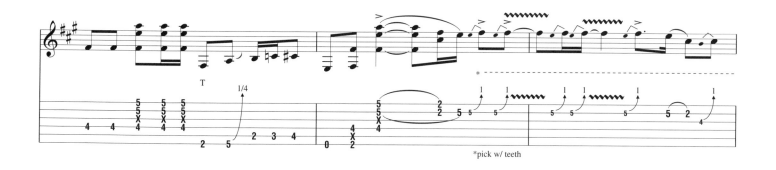

*pick w/ teeth

**Jimi licks strings with his tongue while trilling.

***pick w/ teeth

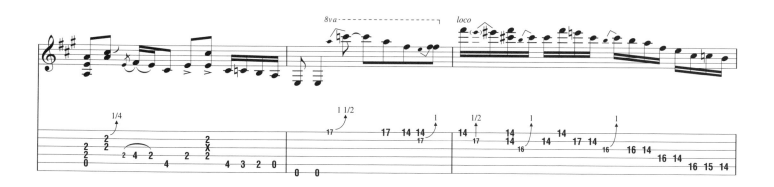

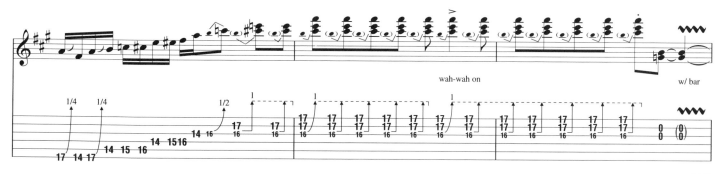

wah-wah on

w/ bar

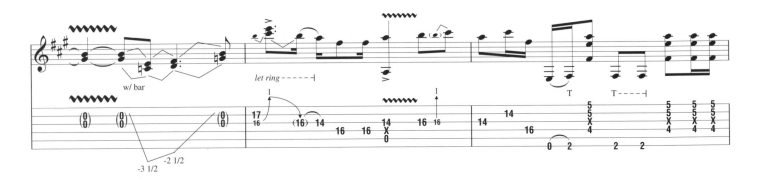

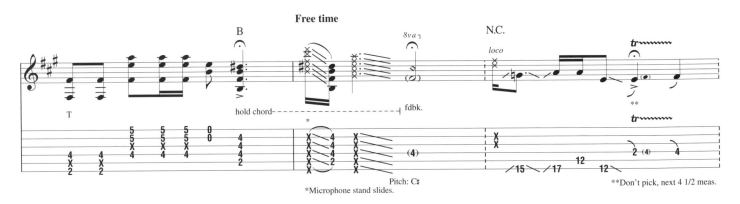

Free time

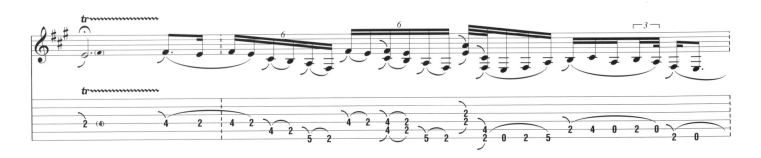

Pitch: C♯

*Microphone stand slides.

**Don't pick, next 4 1/2 meas.

***Bend string behind nut.

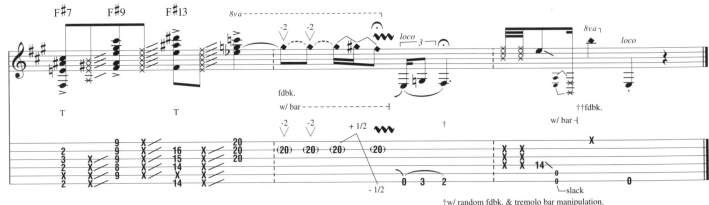

†w/ random fdbk. & tremolo bar manipulation.

††Microphonic fdbk.,
not caused by string vibration.

Message to Love
(Message of Love)
Words and Music by Jimi Hendrix

*"Y'all wanna hear all those old songs, man? Damn, man, we're just tryin' to get some other things together.
I just woke up about two minutes ago. We was recording some little things, but I don't think, uh...I don't know. I think we'll play something
a little more familiar. 'Cause I ain't came yet, myself, I don't know about you but I ain't came yet. There, I came, thank you very much, good night."*

Tune down 1/2 step:
(low to high) E♭-A♭-D♭-G♭-B♭-E♭

Intro

Moderate Rock ♩ = 112

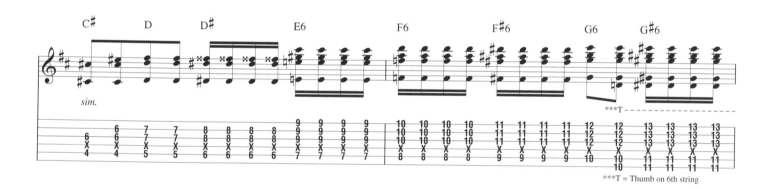

*Chord symbols reflect implied harmony.

**Jimi tunes up G string.

***T = Thumb on 6th string

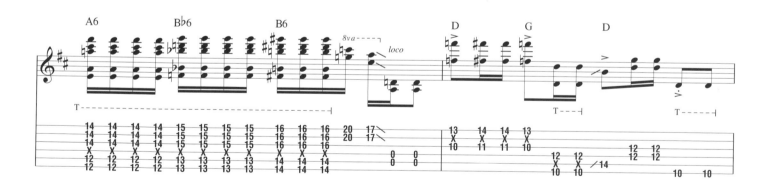

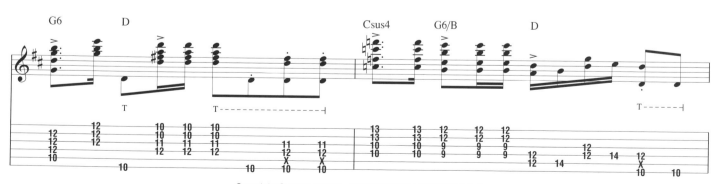

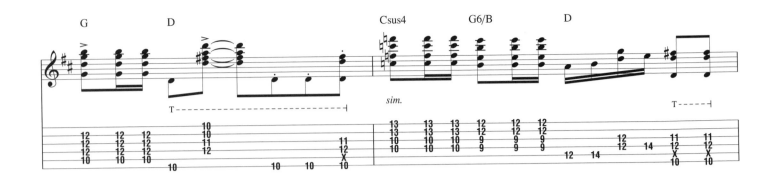

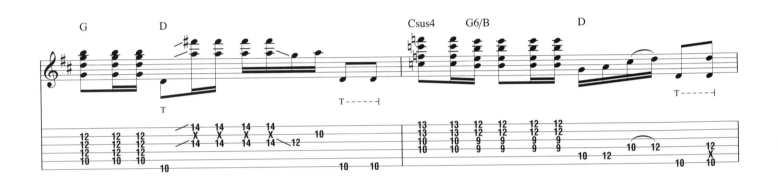

Verse

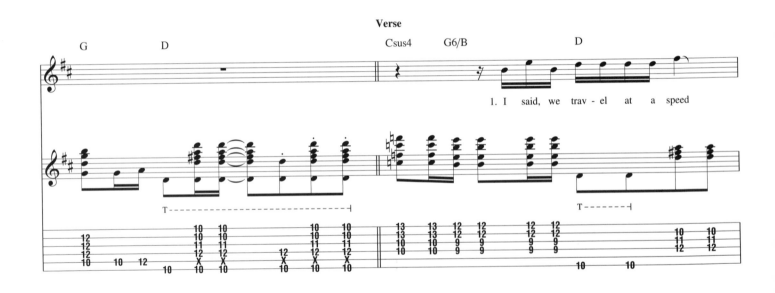

1. I said, we trav-el at a speed

of a re-born man. ___ Got-ta lot of love ___ to give

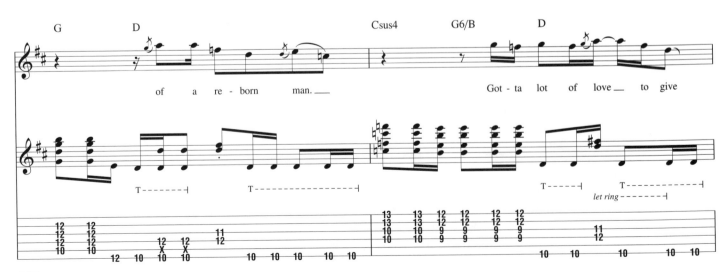

from the mir-rors in my hand.

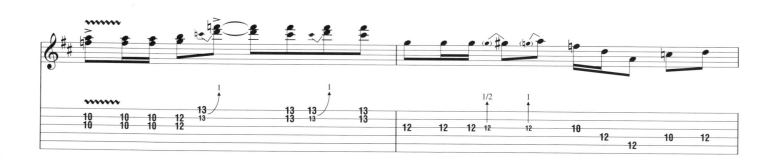

Verse

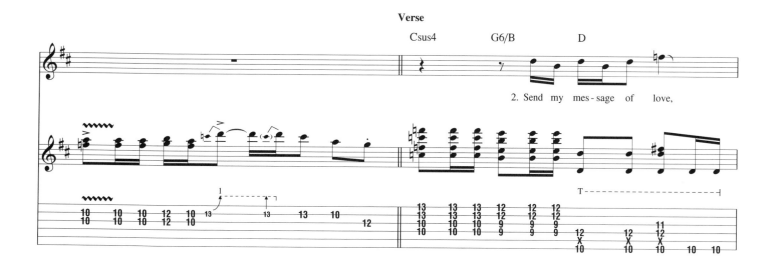

2. Send my mes-sage of love,

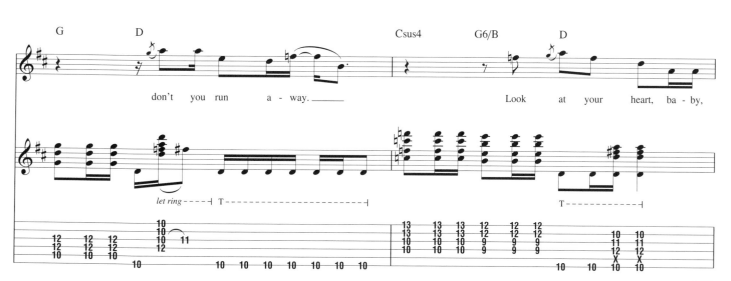

don't you run a - way.＿＿＿ Look at your heart, ba - by,

144

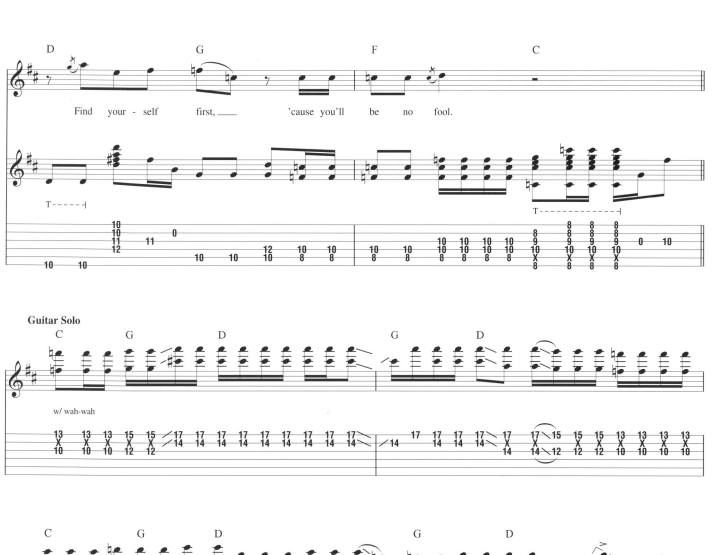

Find your-self first, ____ 'cause you'll be no fool.

Guitar Solo

w/ wah-wah

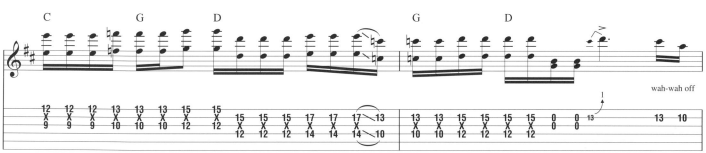

wah-wah off

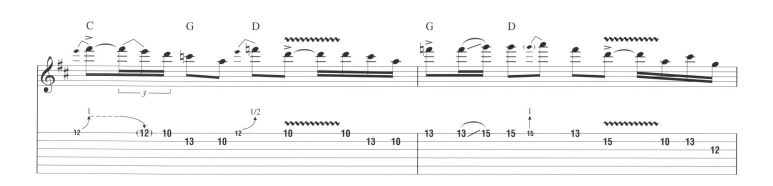

grad. bend

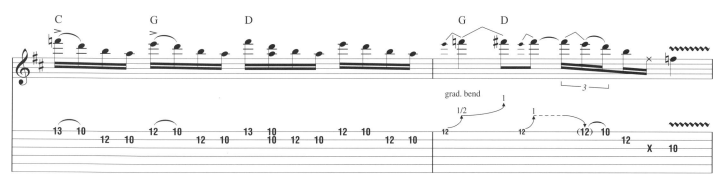

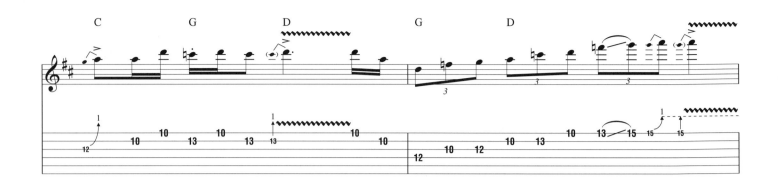

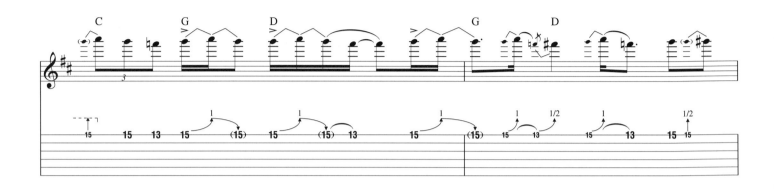

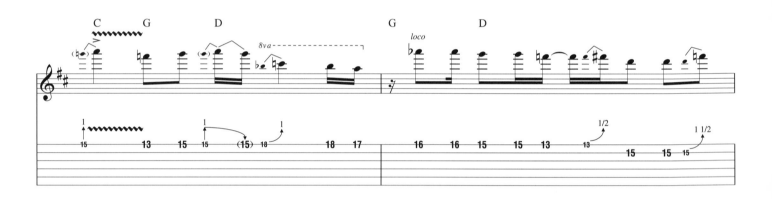

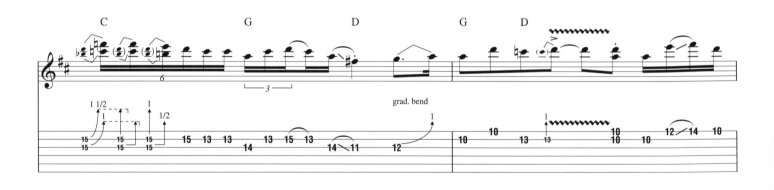

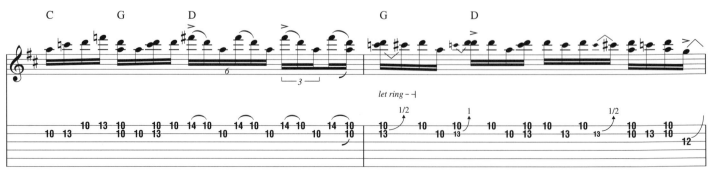

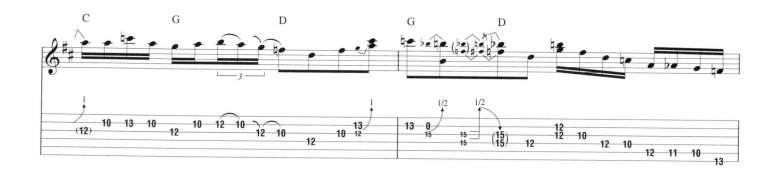

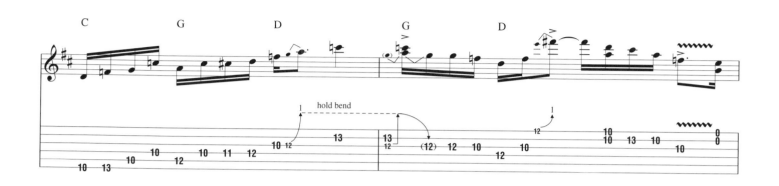

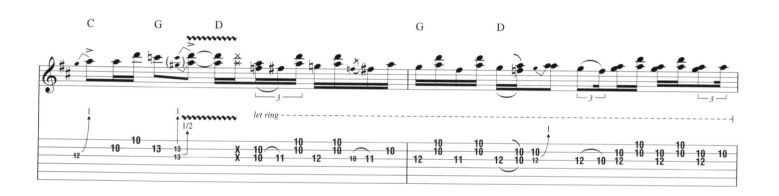

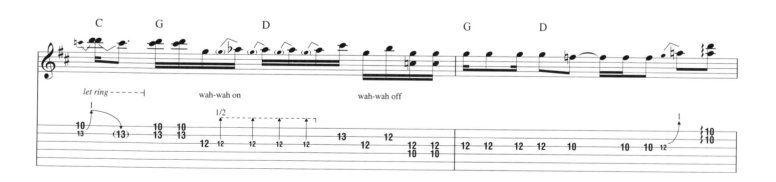

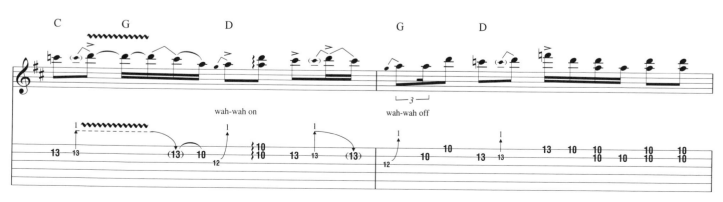

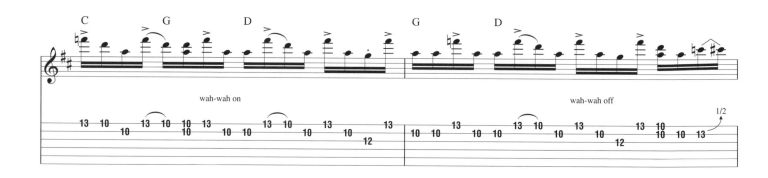

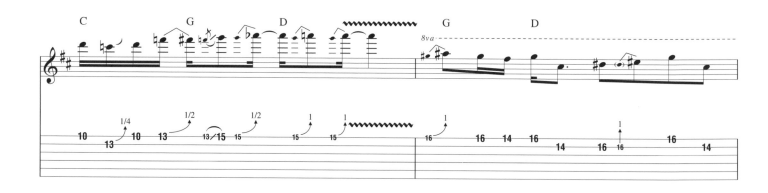

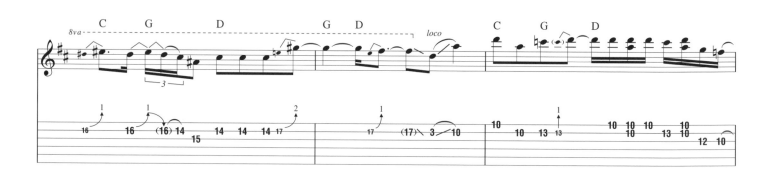

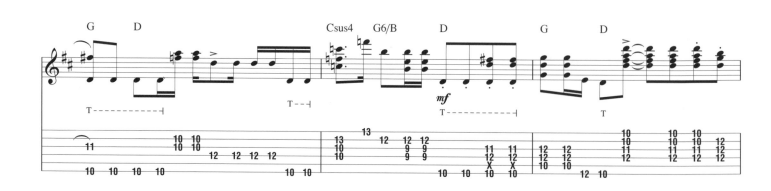

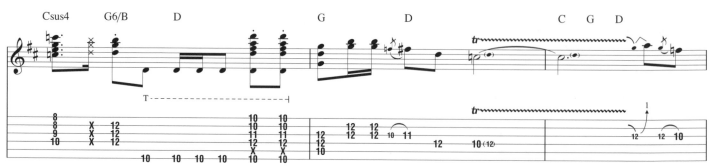

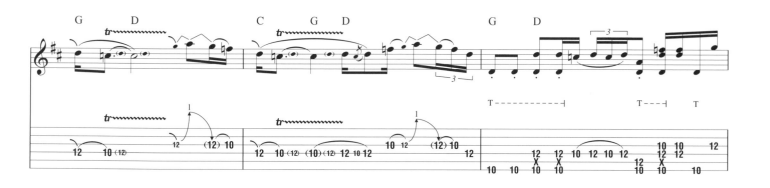

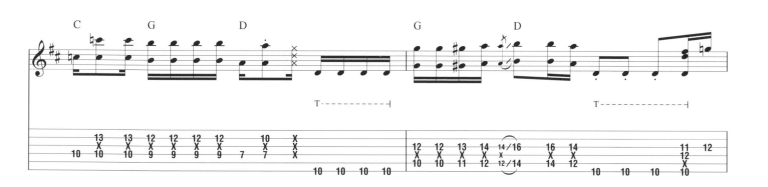

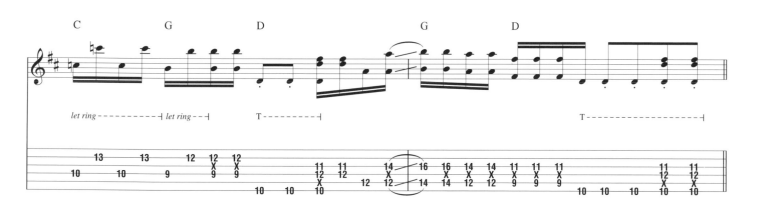

Verse

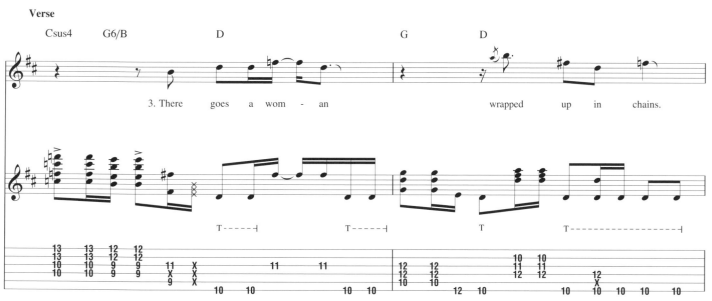

3. There goes a wom-an wrapped up in chains.

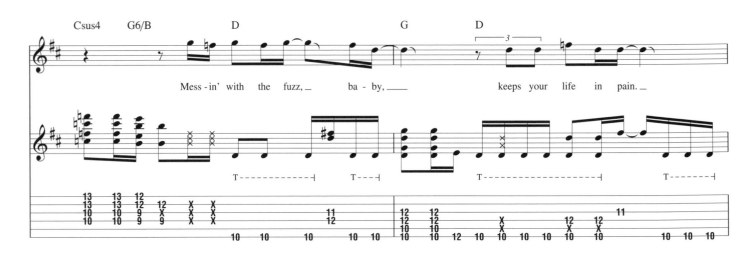

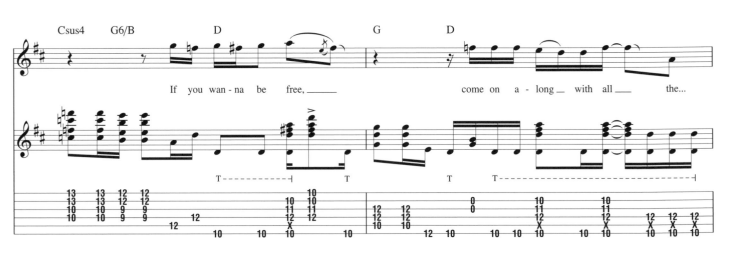

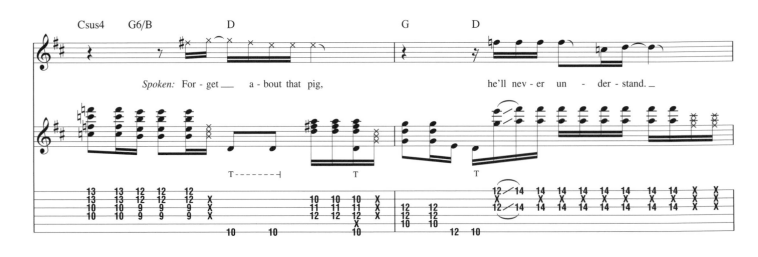

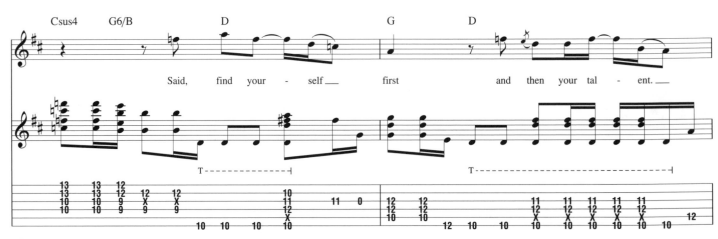

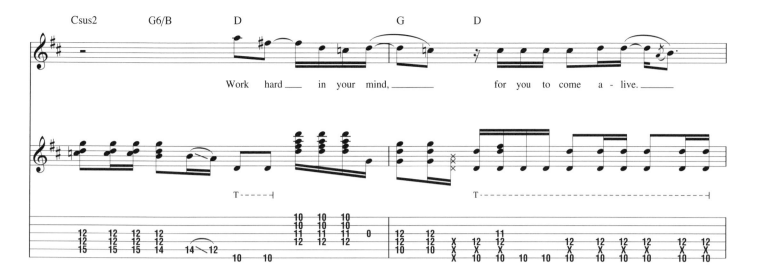

Work hard ____ in your mind, ____ for you to come a-live. ____

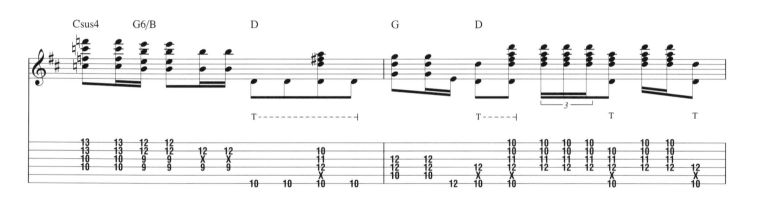

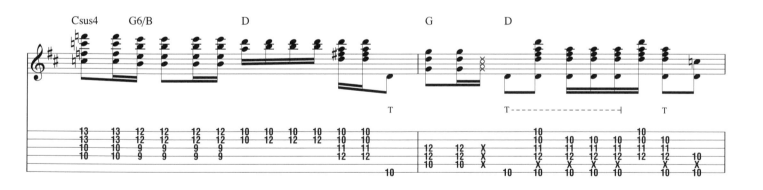

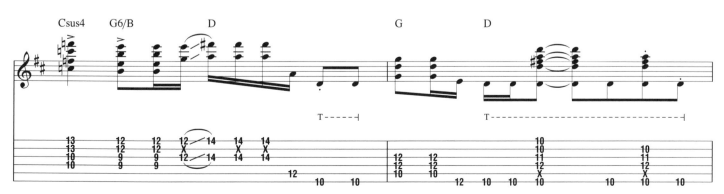

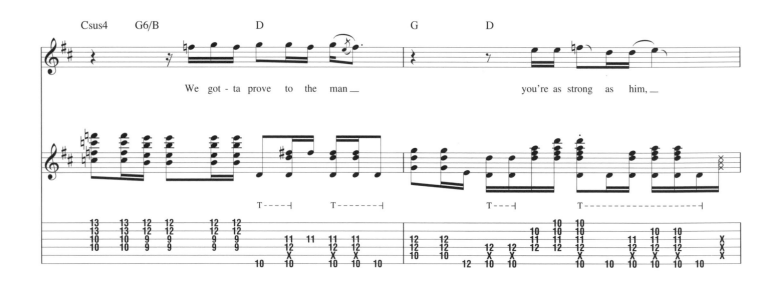

We got-ta prove to the man __ you're as strong as him, __

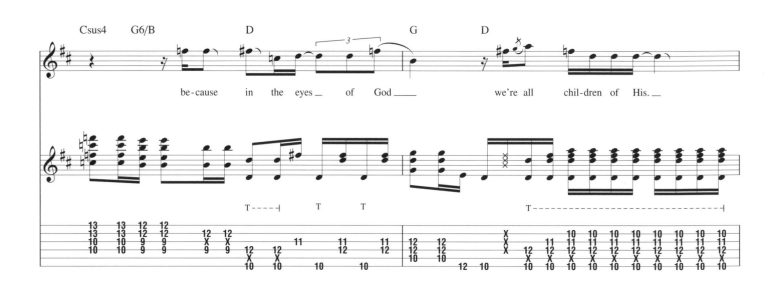

be-cause in the eyes __ of God __ we're all chil-dren of His. __

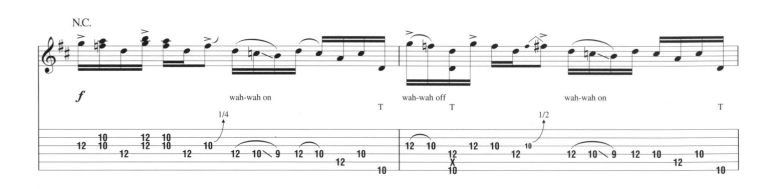

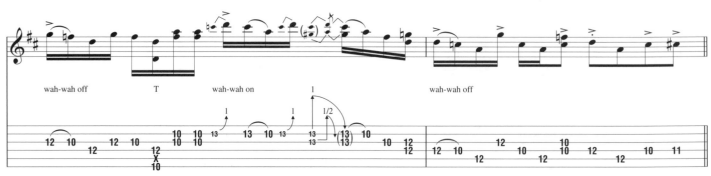

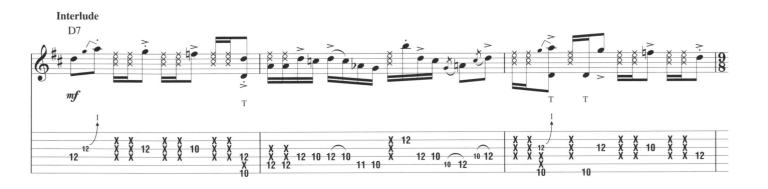

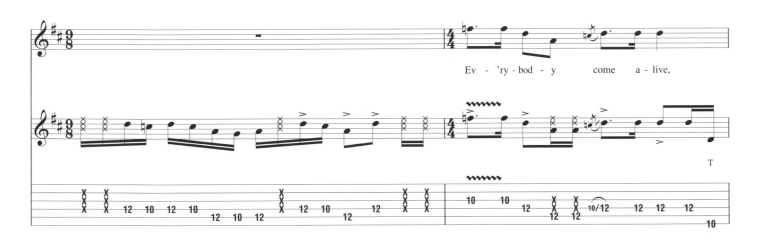

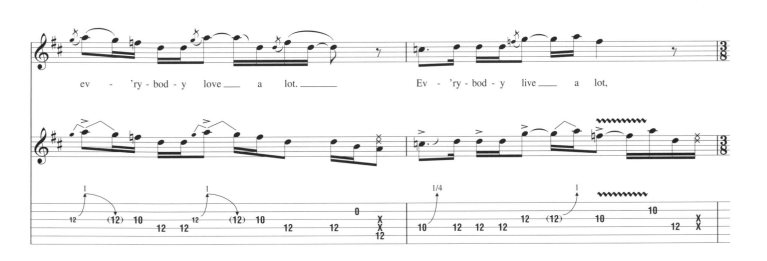

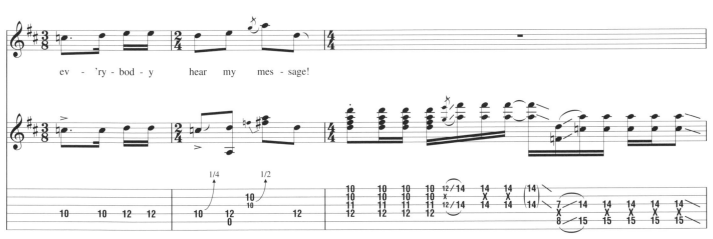

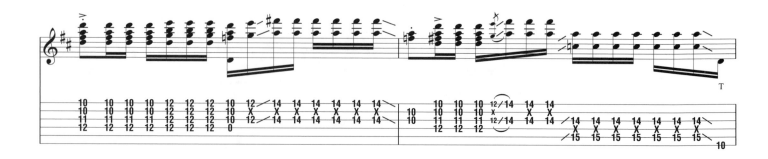

Guitar Solo

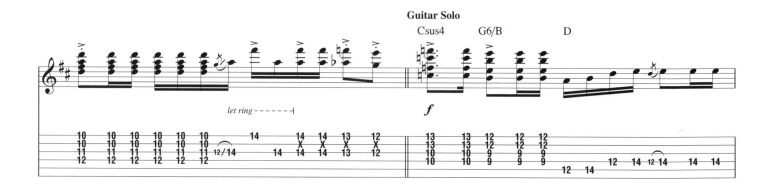

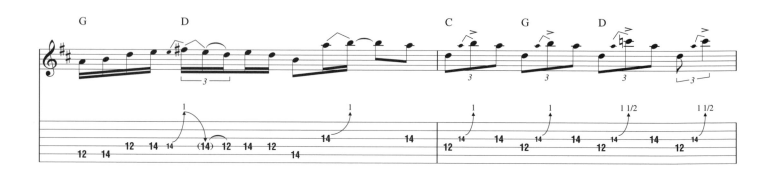

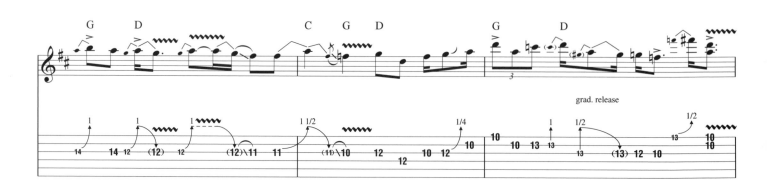

154

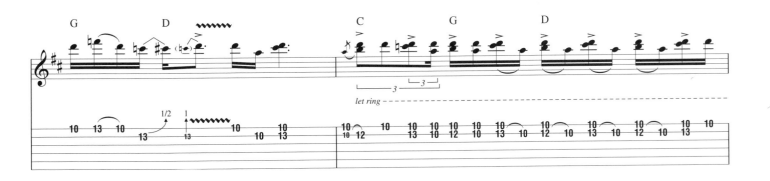

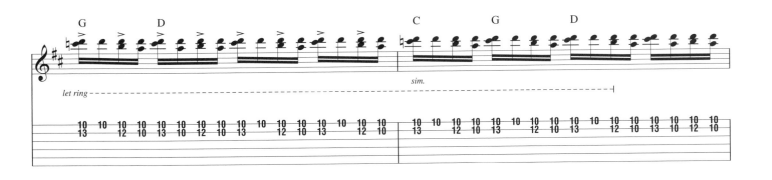

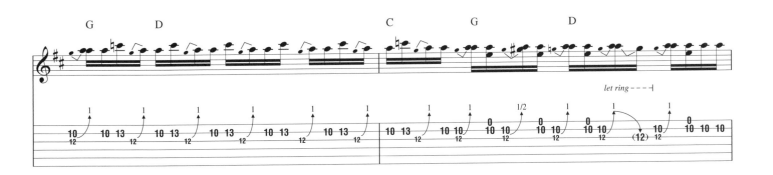

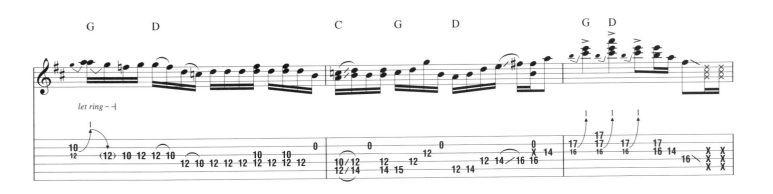

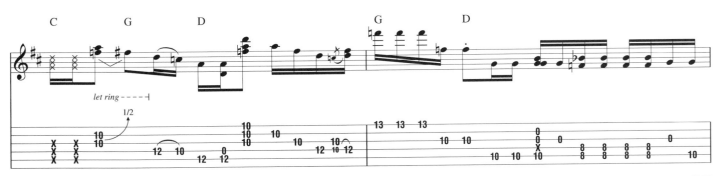

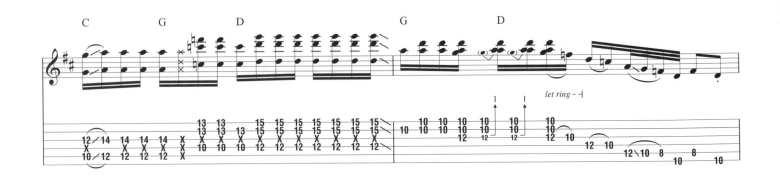

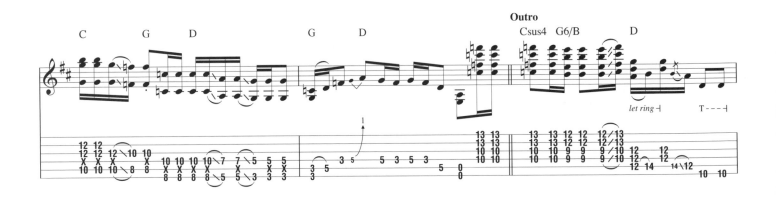

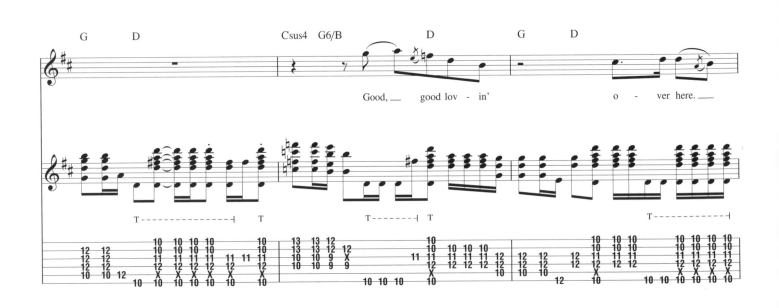

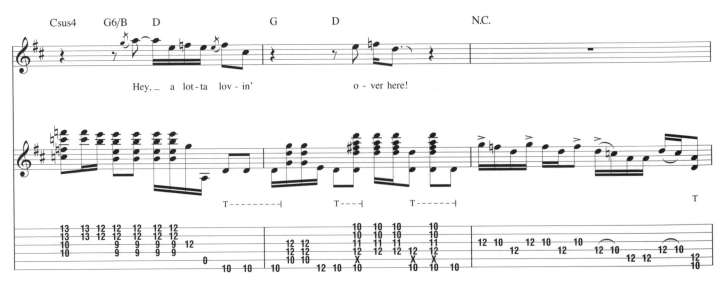

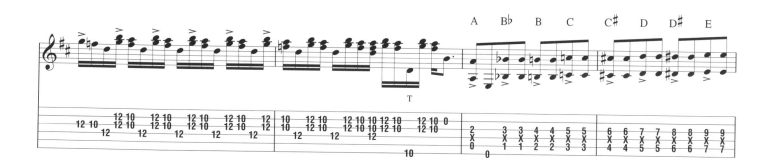

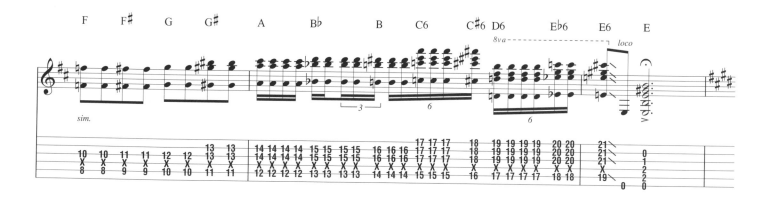

Free time

Segue to "Hey Baby (New Rising Sun)"

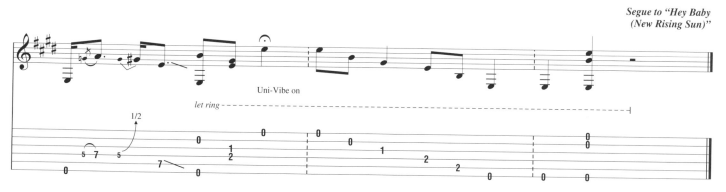

Hey Baby
(New Rising Sun)
Words and Music by Jimi Hendrix

Tune down 1/2 step:
(low to high) E♭-A♭-D♭-G♭-B♭-E♭

Intro
Free time

N.C.

Gtr. 1 (dist.)

mf
w/ Uni-Vibe

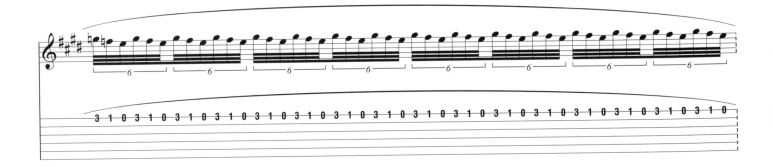

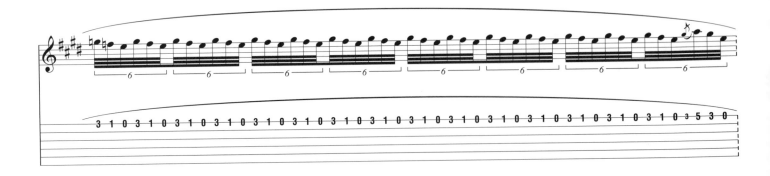

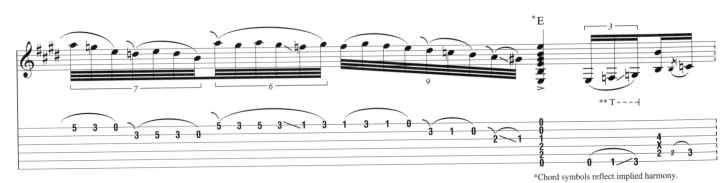

*Chord symbols reflect implied harmony.

**T = Thumb on 6th string

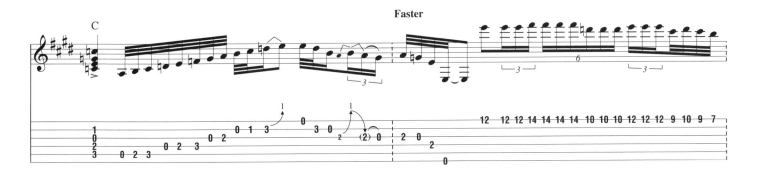

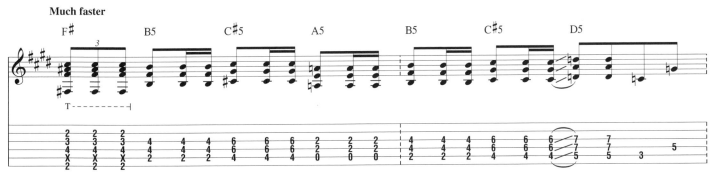

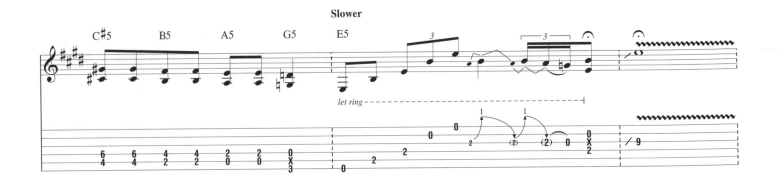

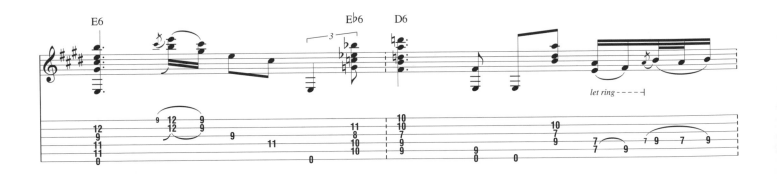

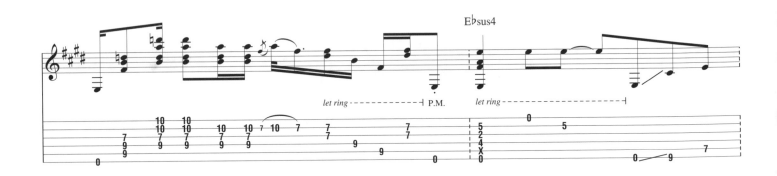

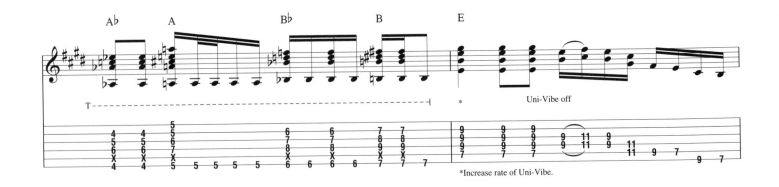

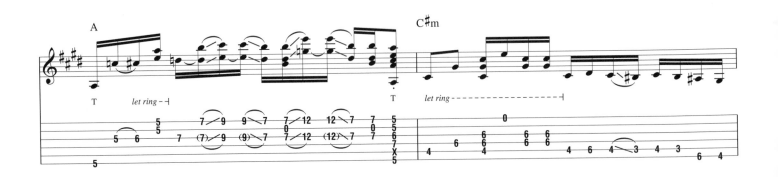

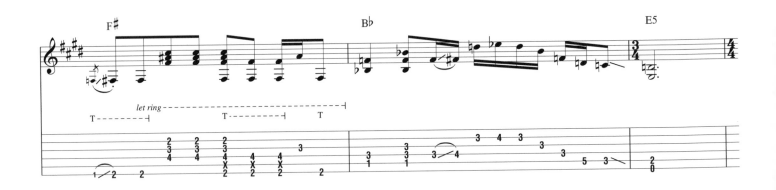

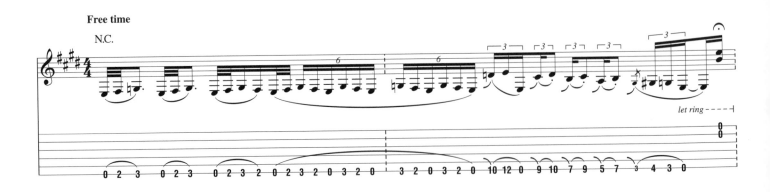

162

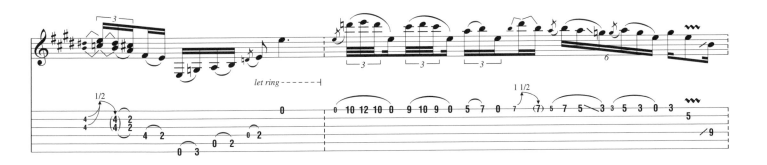

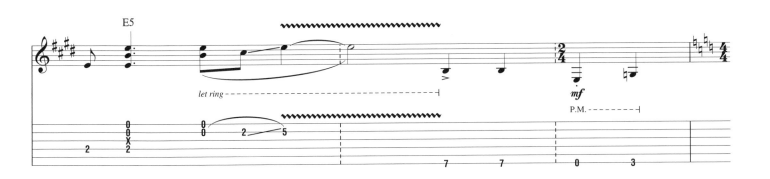

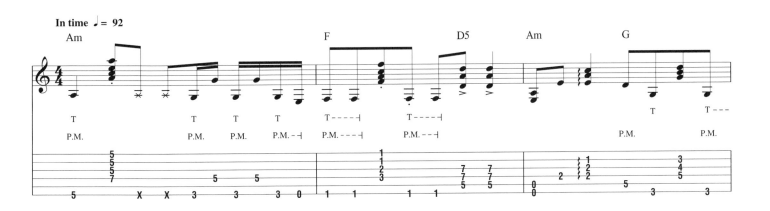

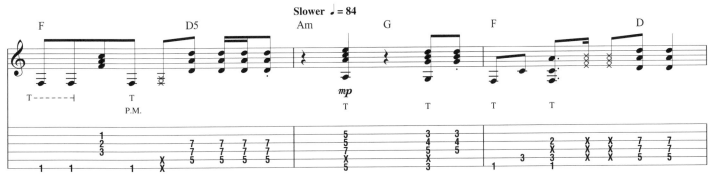

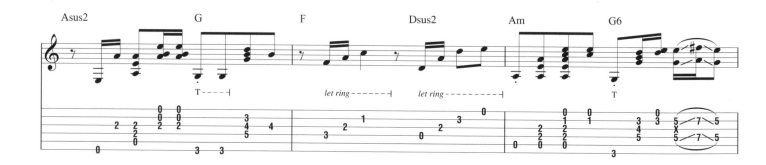

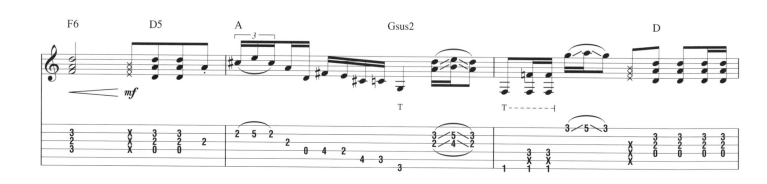

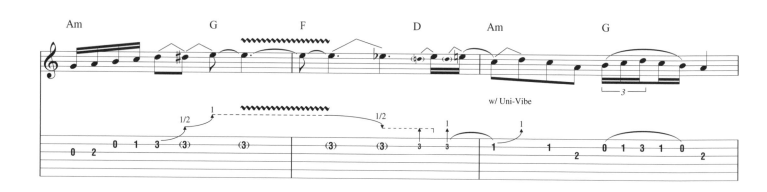

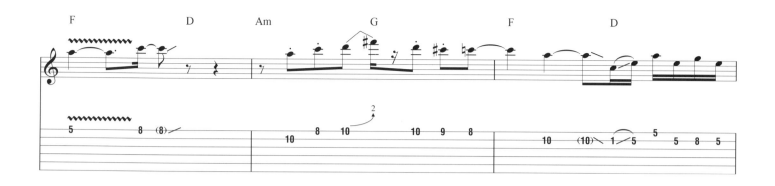

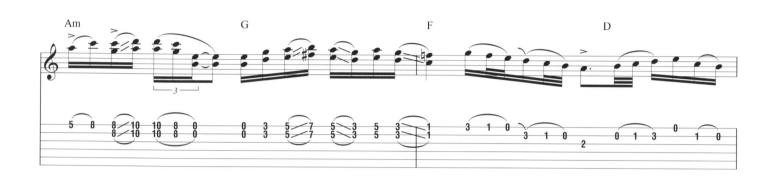

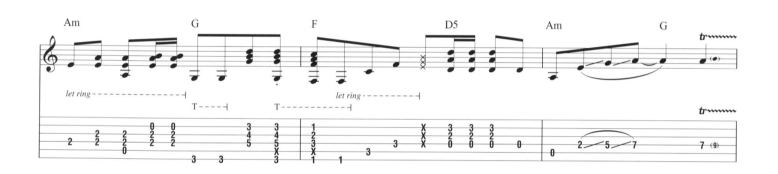

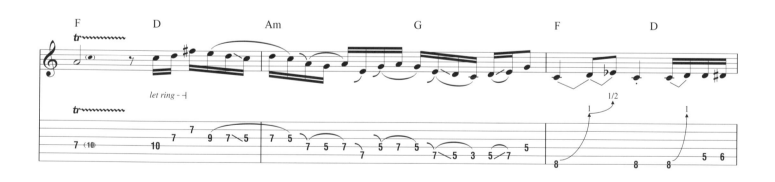

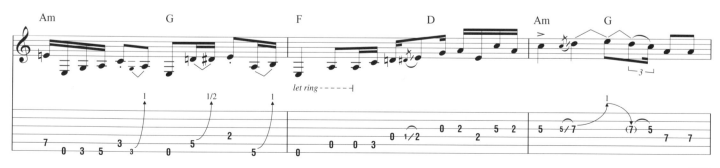

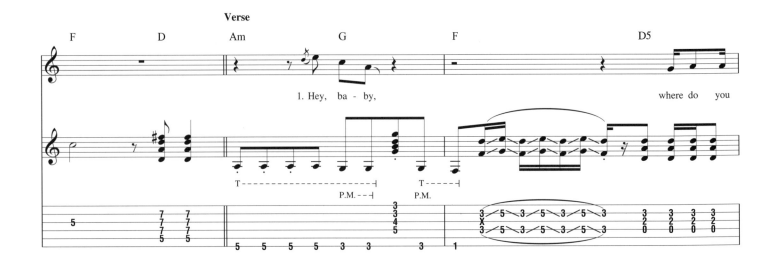

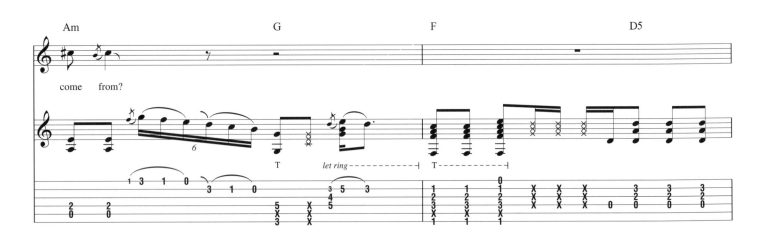

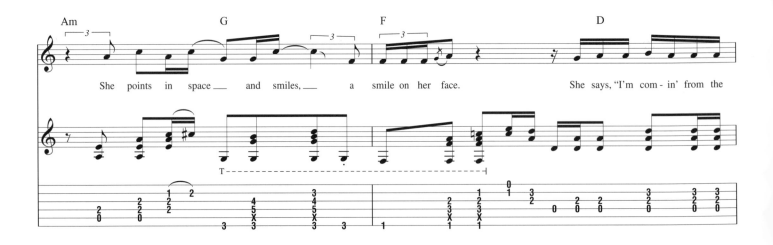

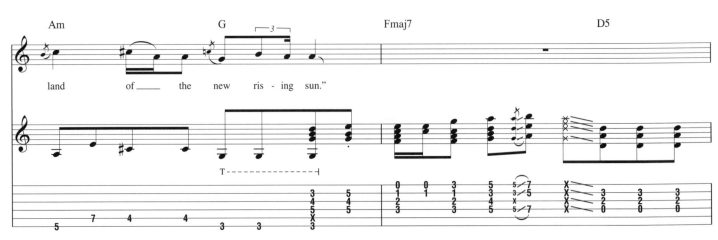

Chorus

May I come a-long? _____   May I come a-long? _____

May I come a-long, _____ ba-by,

yeah?   Please _____ take me, oh.

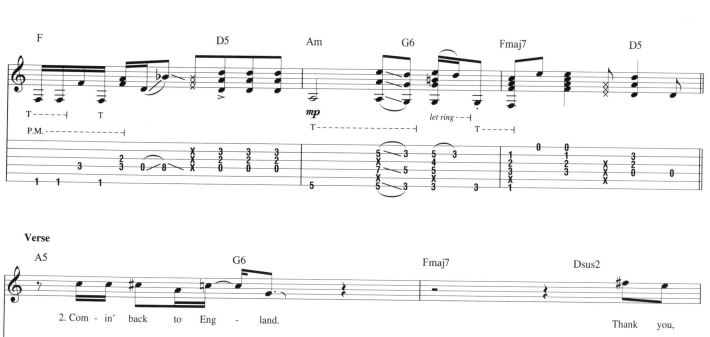

Verse

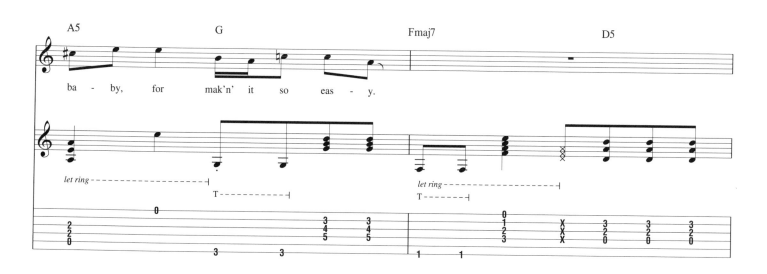

2. Com - in' back to Eng - land. Thank you,

ba - by, for mak'n' it so eas - y.

Go - in' through chang - es in New York, Chi - ca - go.

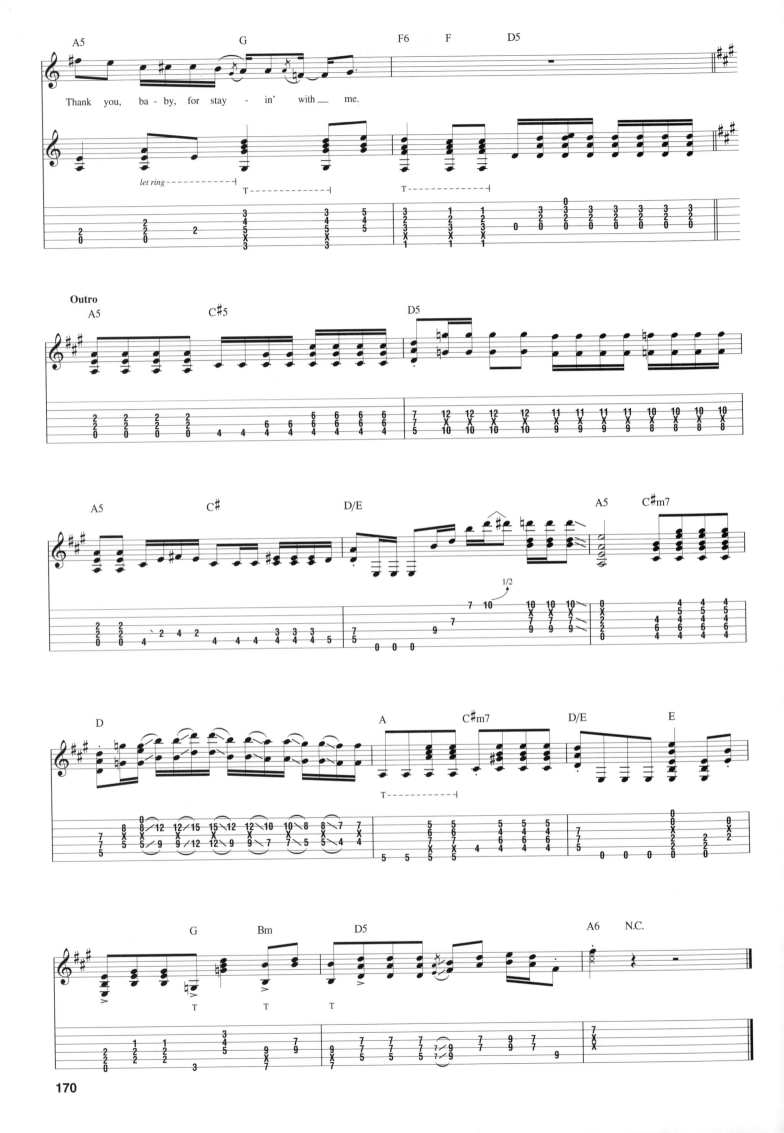

Thank you, ba - by, for stay - in' with ___ me.

EZY Ryder

Words and Music by Jimi Hendrix

Tune down 1/2 step:
(low to high) Eb-Ab-Db-Gb-Bb-Eb

Intro

Moderate Rock ♩ = 144

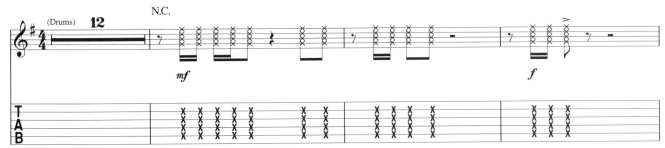

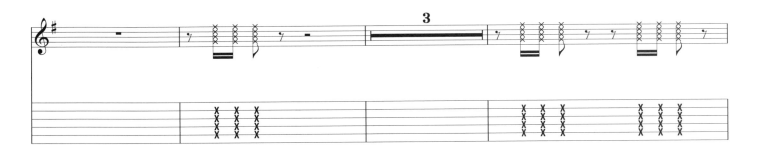

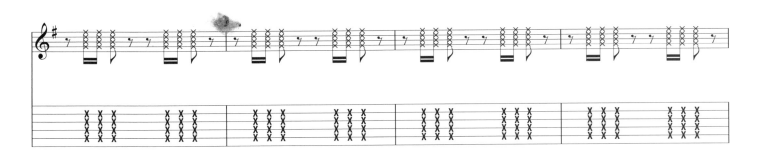

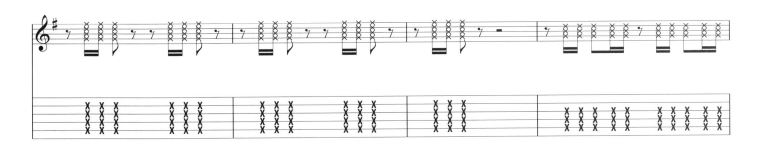

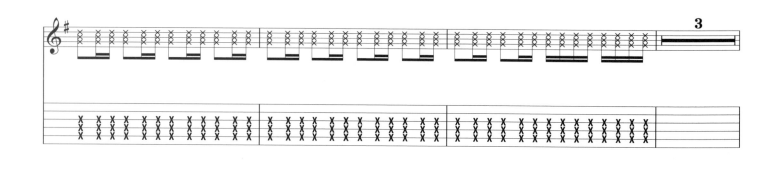

w/ wah-wah

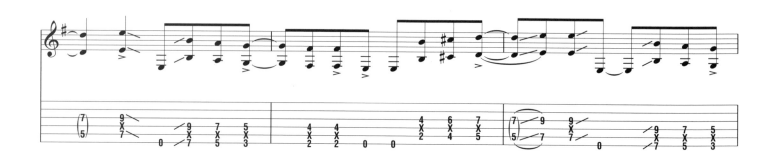

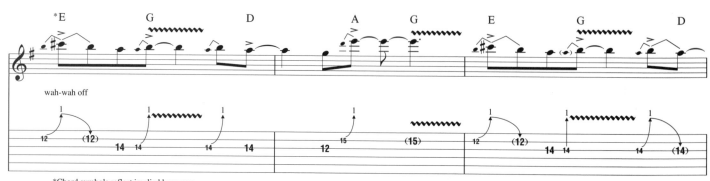

wah-wah off

*Chord symbols reflect implied harmony.

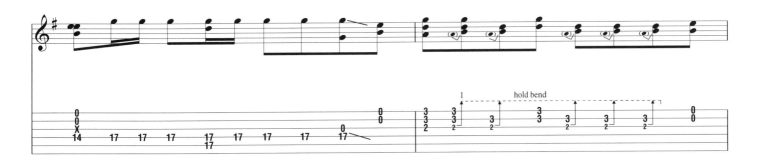

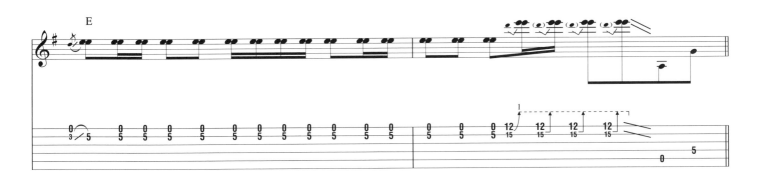

Interlude

Bridge

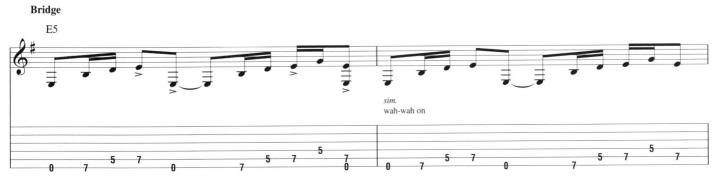

mar - ry me?

Got me stone _____

_____ cra - zy.

Interlude

N.C.

Guitar Solo

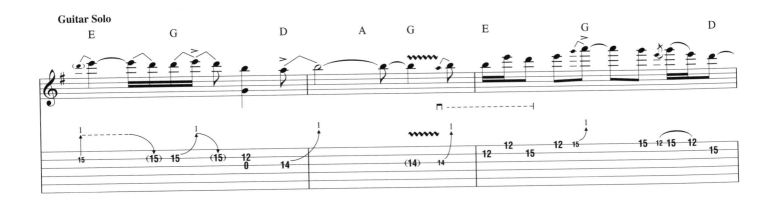

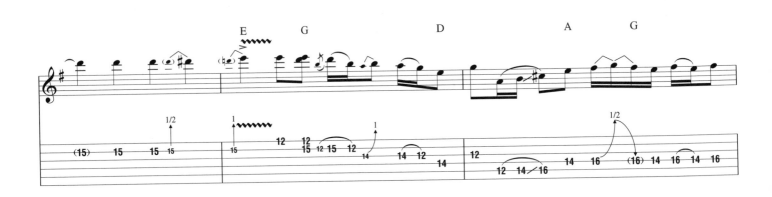

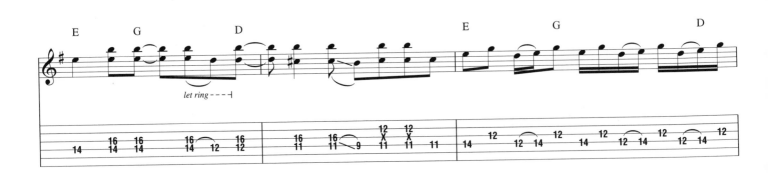

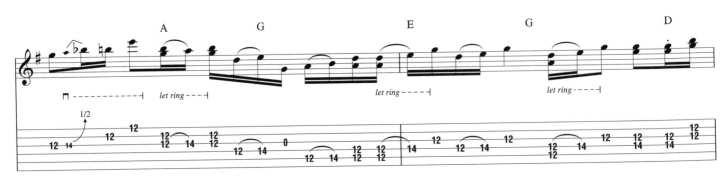

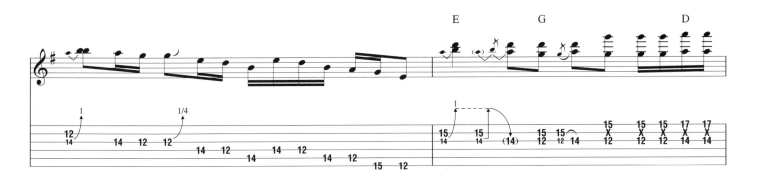

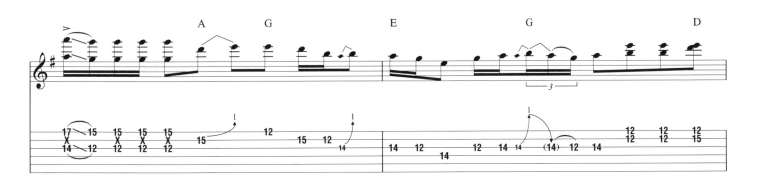

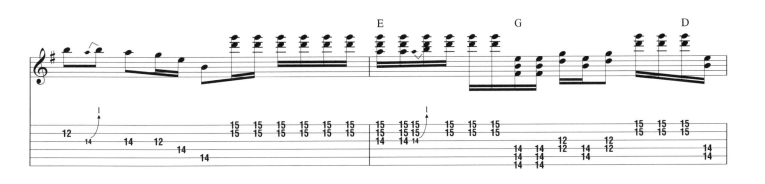

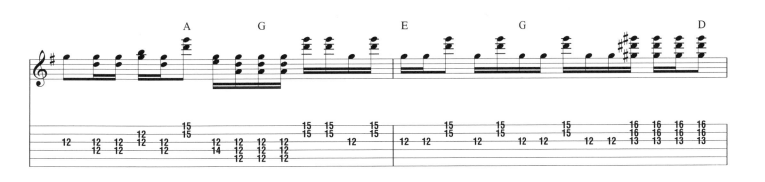

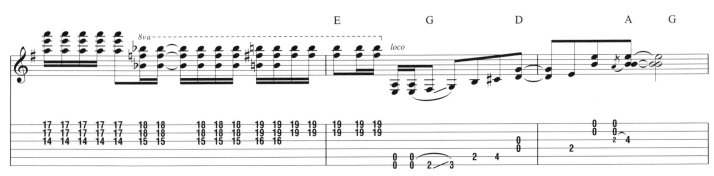

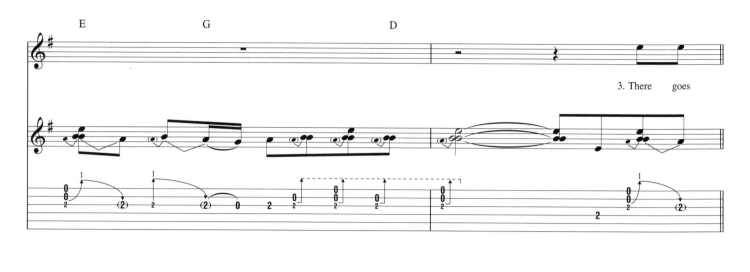

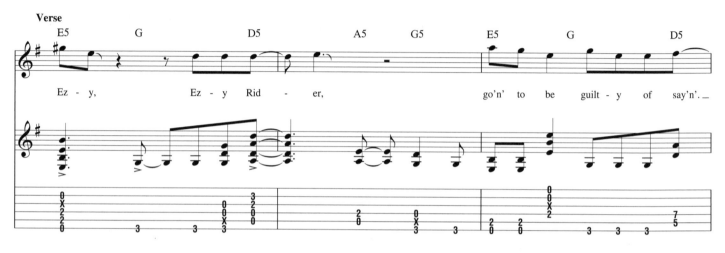

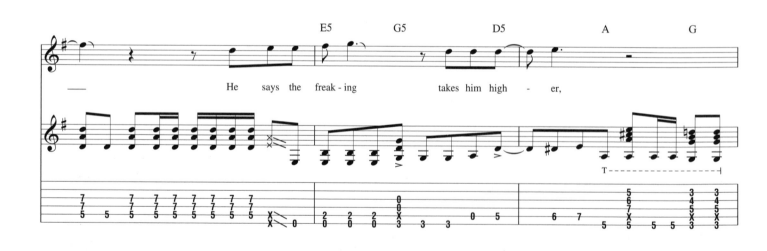

Throw - in' a - way ___ his dream. ___ Here comes

Ez - y Rid - er! Here ___ comes Ez - y Rid - er!

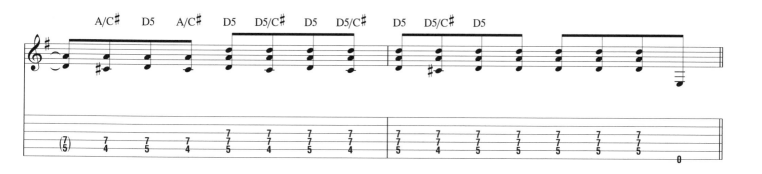

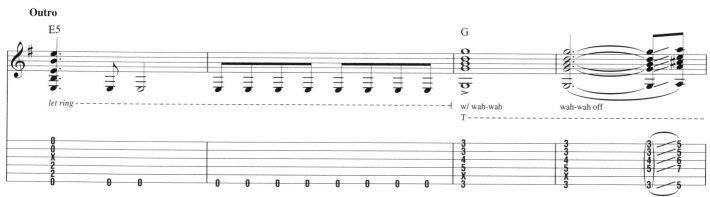

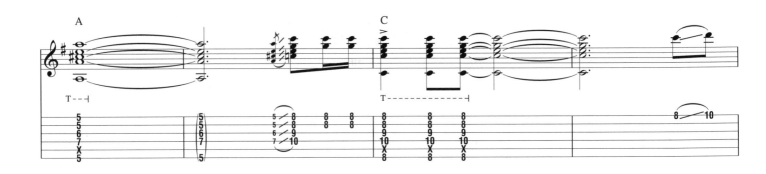

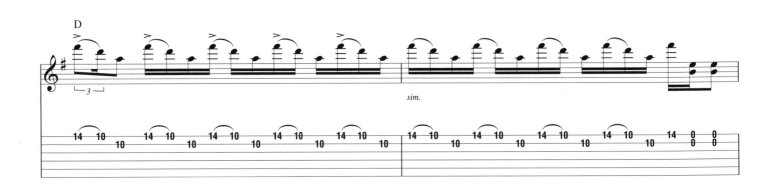

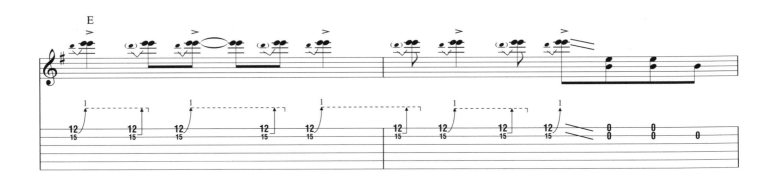

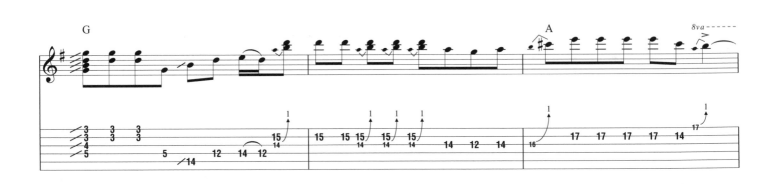

Segue to "Hey Joe"

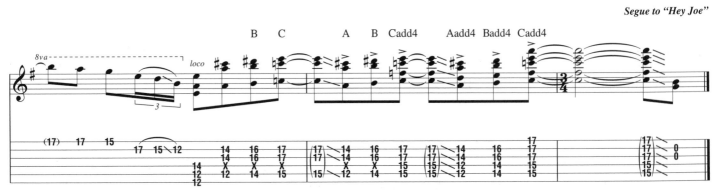

Hey Joe

Words and Music by Billy Roberts

Tune down 1/2 step:
(low to high) Eb-Ab-Db-Gb-Bb-Eb

Intro
Moderately slow ♩ = 76

*Chord symbols reflect basic harmony.

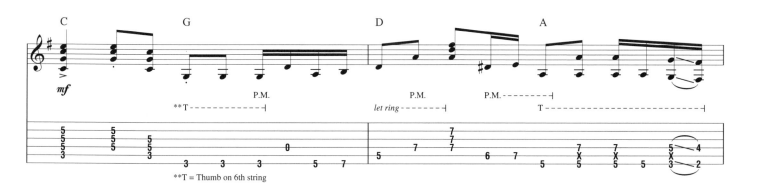

**T = Thumb on 6th string

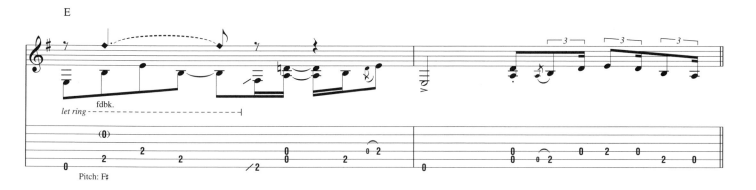

Pitch: F#

Verse

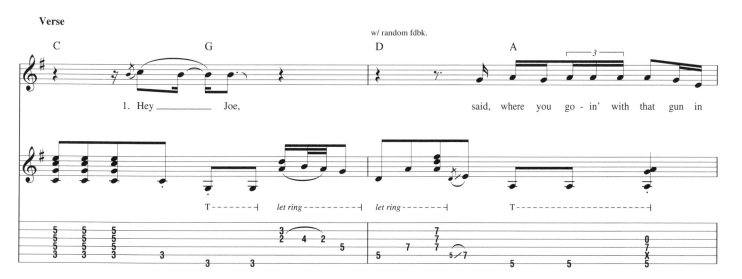

1. Hey _____ Joe, said, where you go-in' with that gun in

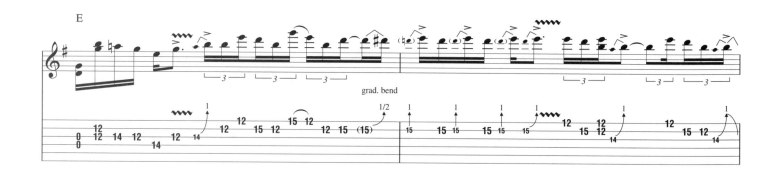

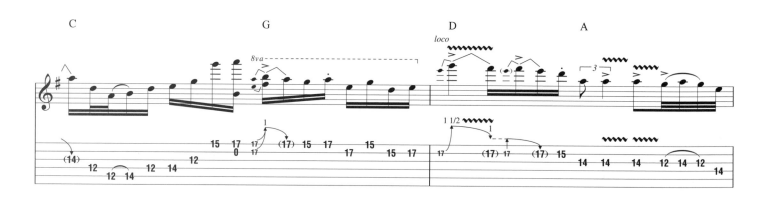

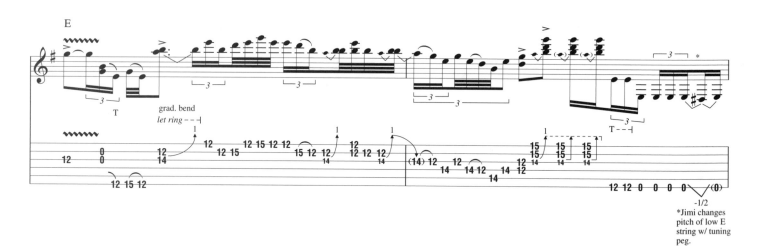

*Jimi changes pitch of low E string w/ tuning peg.

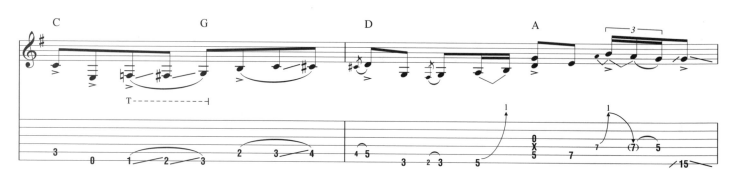

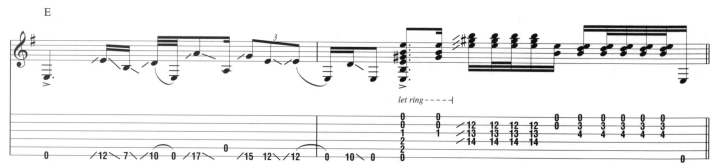

Ain't no red neck hang a, ain't _____ gon - na fool a - round __ with me!

let ring - - - - - - - - - - - - - -   T - - - - - - - - - -   T -

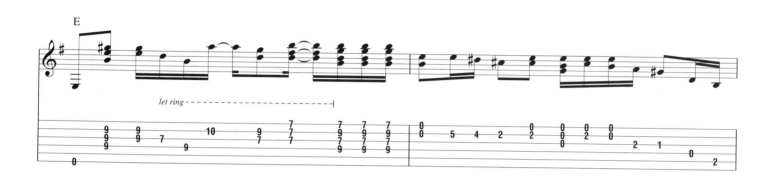

let ring -

Hey, ___ hey ___ Joe,   s'good -

T - - - - - - - - - -

bye, ___ ba - by!   Good - bye!

let ring - - - - -   w/ wah-wah

Outro

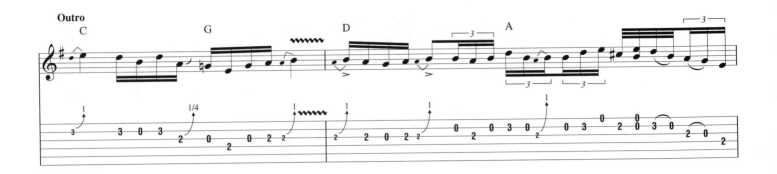

*Played with teeth.

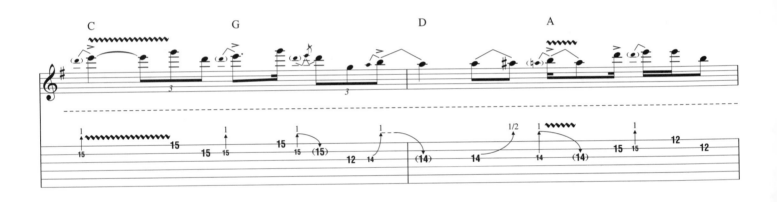

Segue to "Purple Haze"

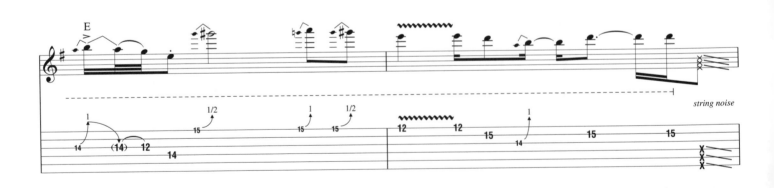

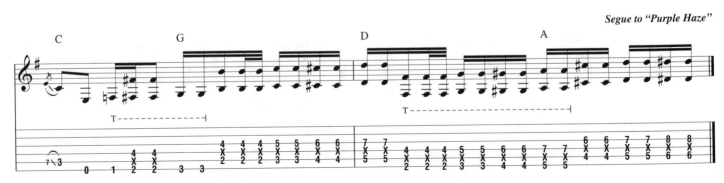

Purple Haze

Words and Music by Jimi Hendrix

Tune down 1/2 step:
(low to high) E♭-A♭-D♭-G♭-B♭-E♭

Intro
Moderate Rock ♩ = 116

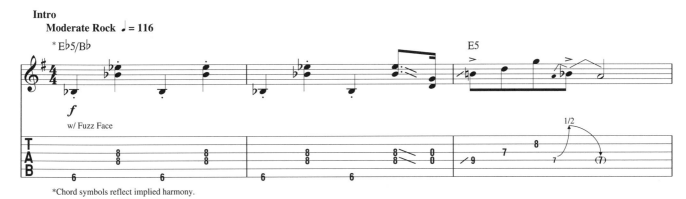

*Chord symbols reflect implied harmony.

w/ Fuzz Face

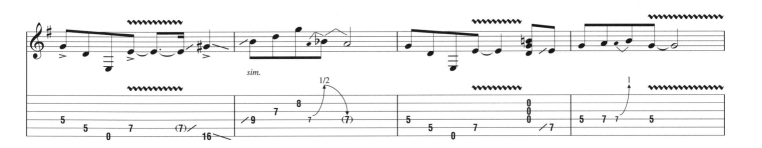

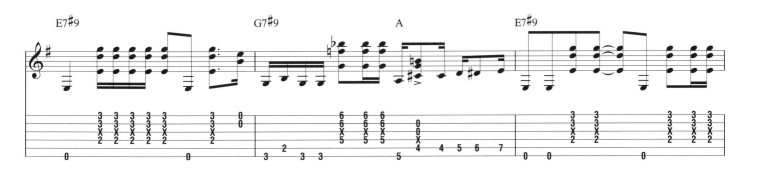

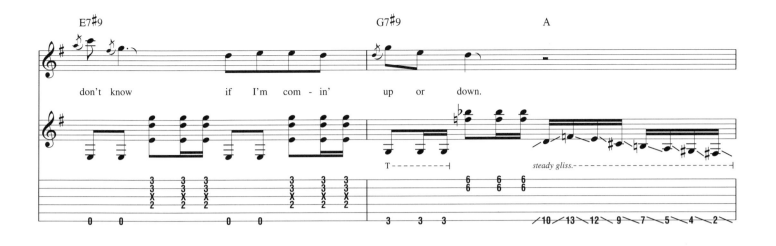

don't know   if I'm com - in'   up or   down.

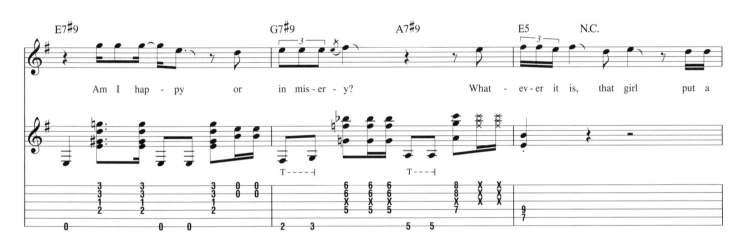

Am I hap - py   or   in mis - er - y?   What - ev - er it is,   that girl   put a

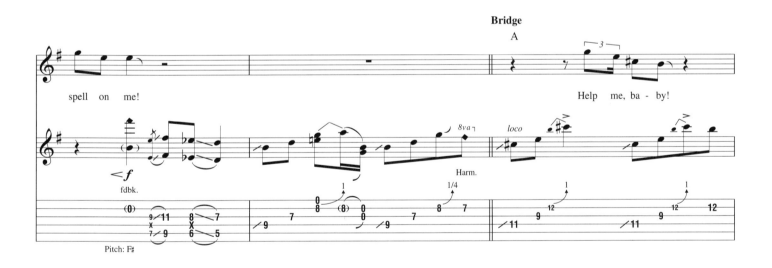

spell on me!   Help   me, ba - by!

Bridge

Pitch: F#

Guitar Solo

For - get   a - bout it, ba - by!

wah-wah on

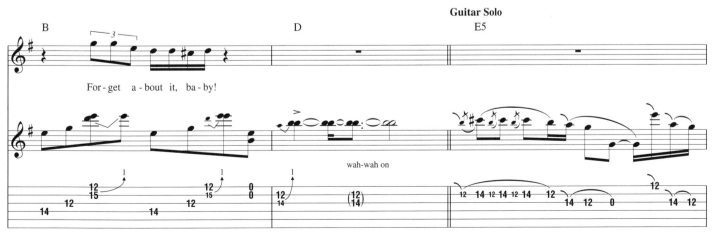

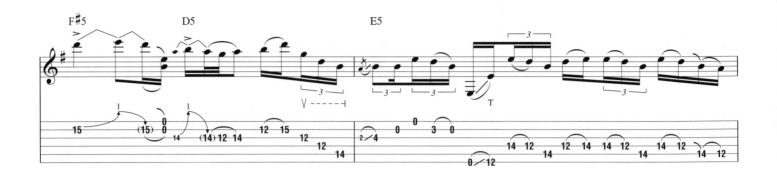

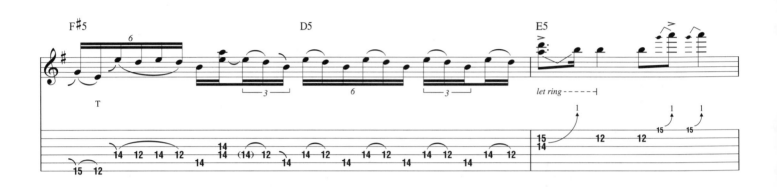

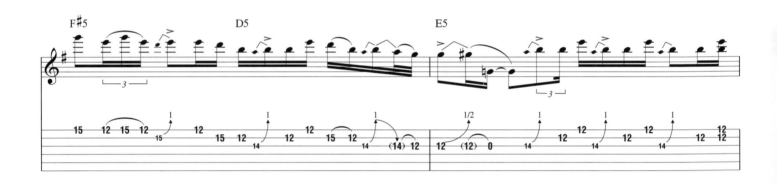

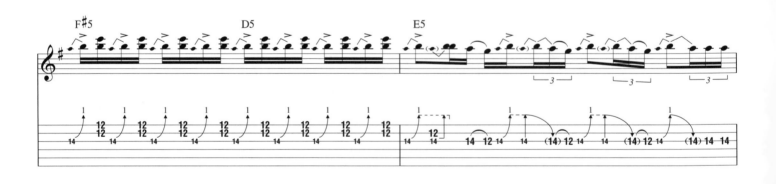

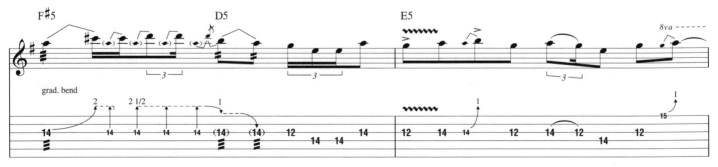

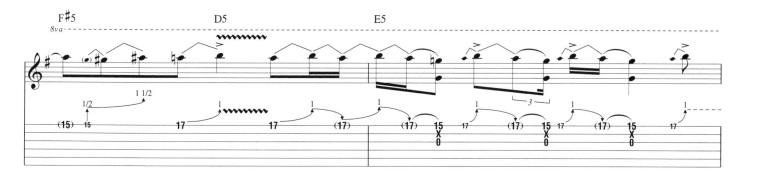

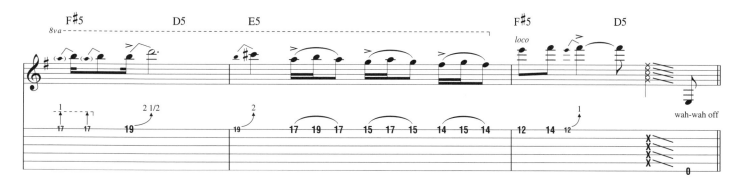

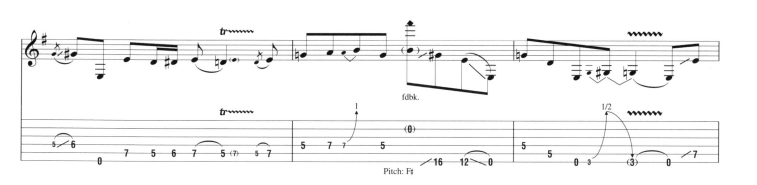

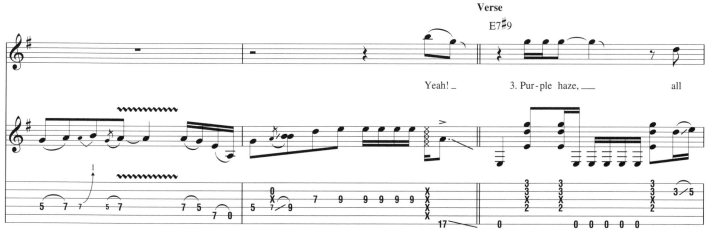

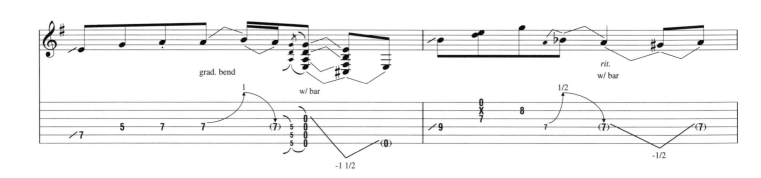

Free time

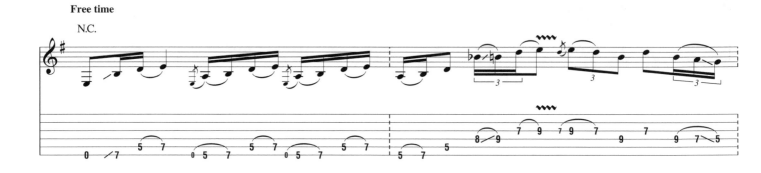

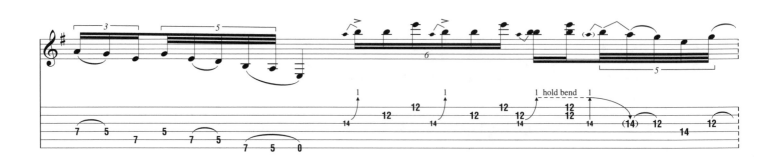

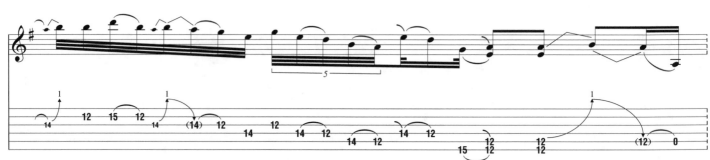

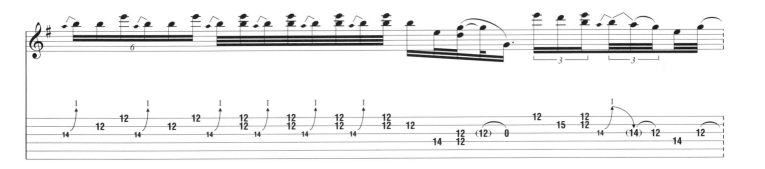

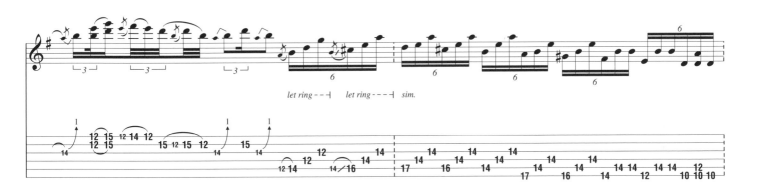

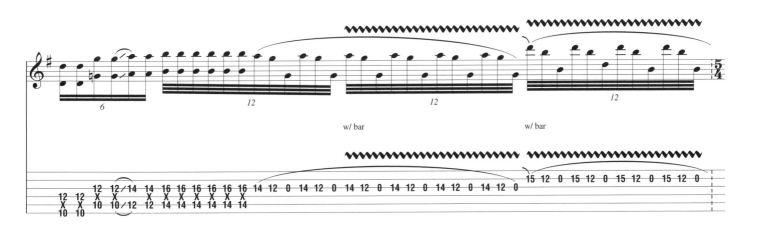

Segue to
"Voodoo Child (Slight Return)"

Voodoo Child
(Slight Return)

Words and Music by Jimi Hendrix

Tune down 1/2 step:
(low to high) Eb-Ab-Db-Gb-Bb-Eb

Intro

Moderate Rock ♩ = 100

*Chord symbols reflect implied harmony.

**B str. tuned sharp accidentally.

***Jimi
corrects tuning
on B string.

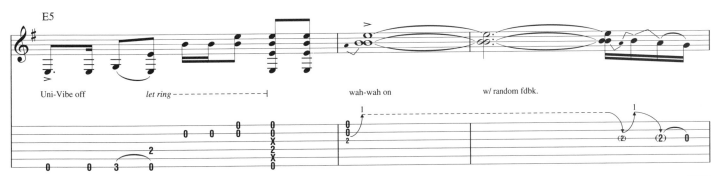

Verse

1. Well, I   stand up next to a moun-tain.

Well, I stand up next to a moun-tain, I chop it down__ with the edge of my

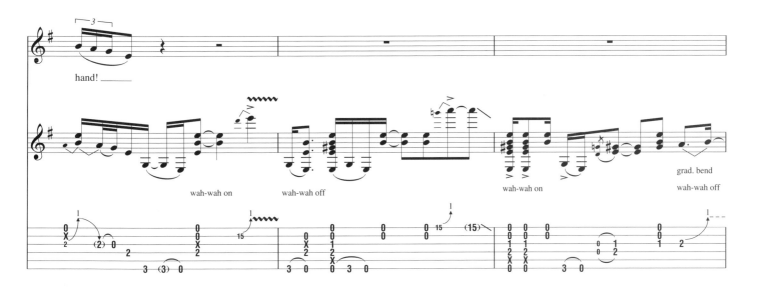

hand!_____

wah-wah on　　wah-wah off　　　　　　　wah-wah on　　　　wah-wah off

Well, I stand up next to a moun-tain, I chop it down__ with the edge of my

on off on off

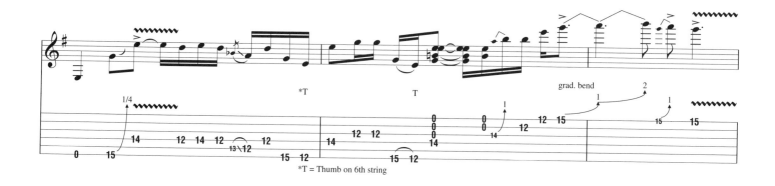

*T = Thumb on 6th string

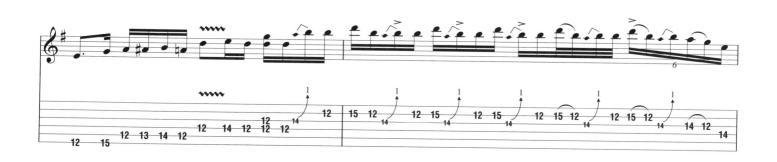

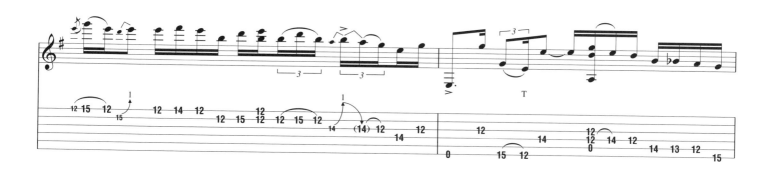

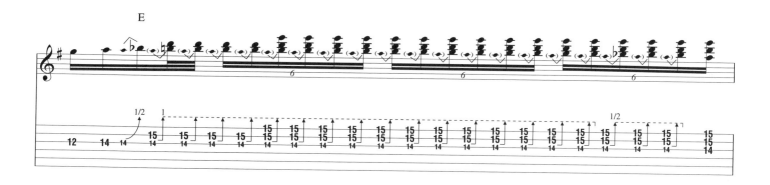

E

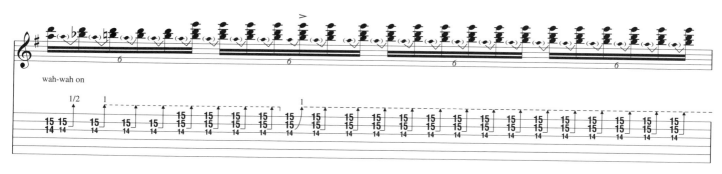

wah-wah on

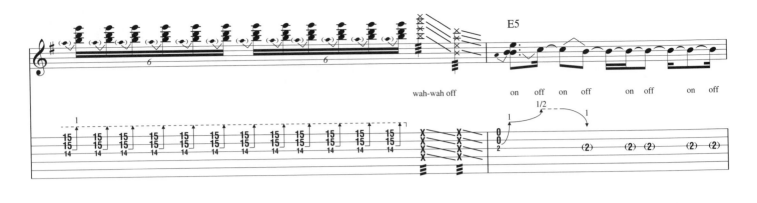

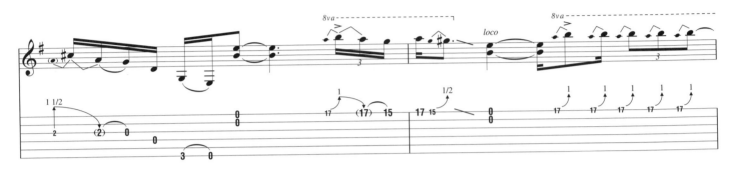

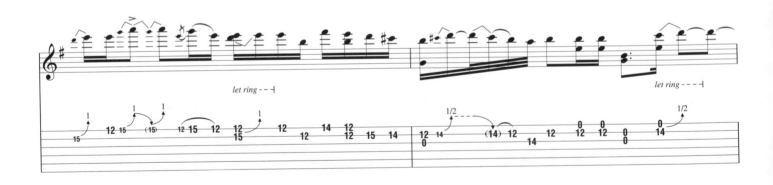

208

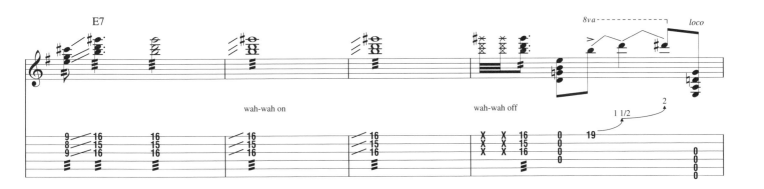

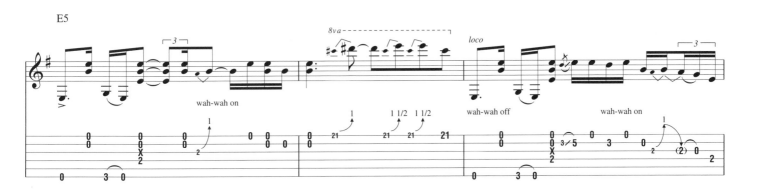

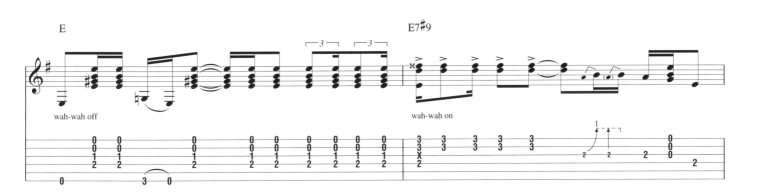

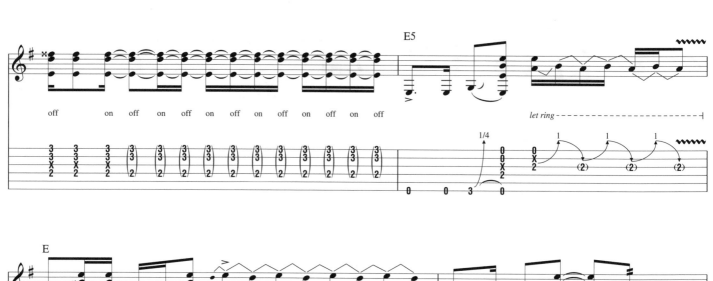

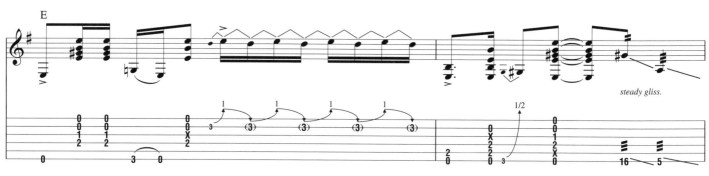

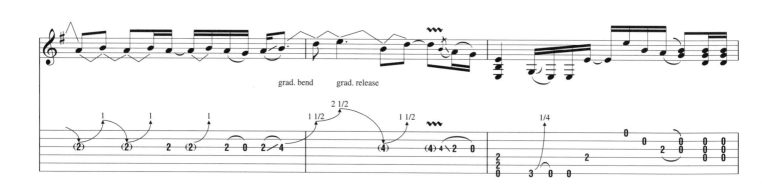

2. I did-n't

see you no more in this world, ___ Lord, I'll meet you on the next one and don't be

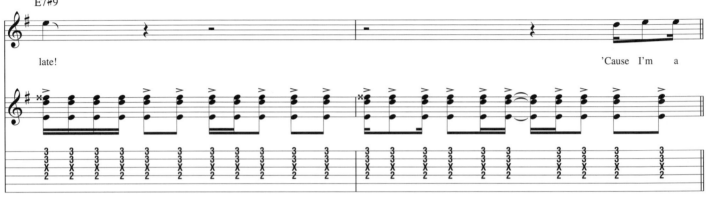

late! 'Cause I'm a

Chorus

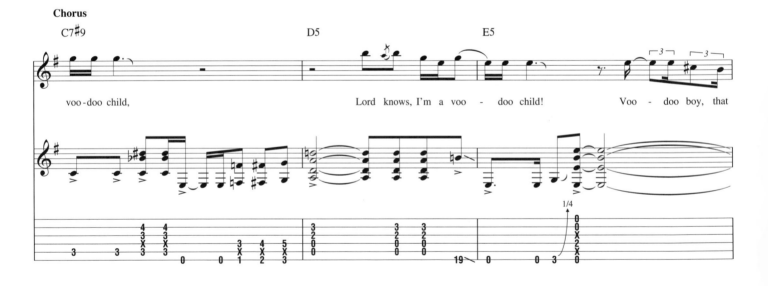

voo-doo child, Lord knows, I'm a voo - doo child! Voo - doo boy, that

Guitar Solo

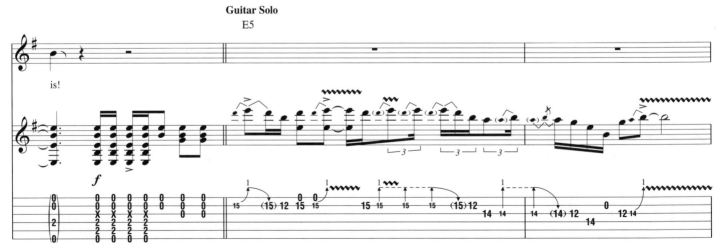

is!

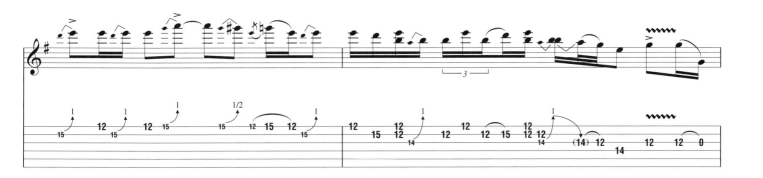

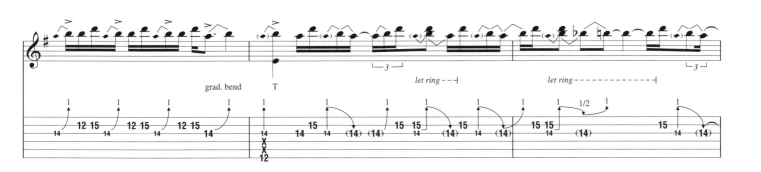

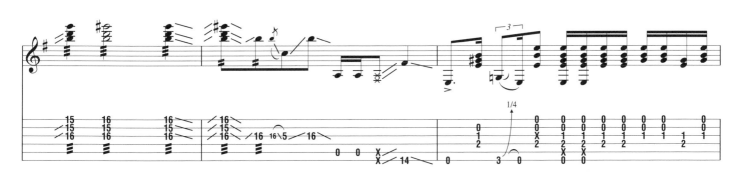

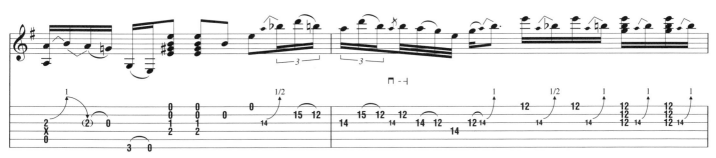

Pitch: A

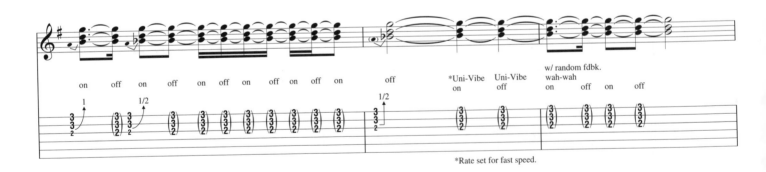

*Rate set for fast speed.

216

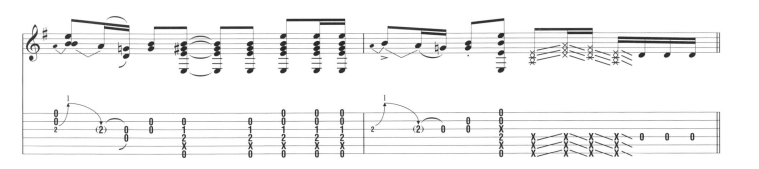

Outro

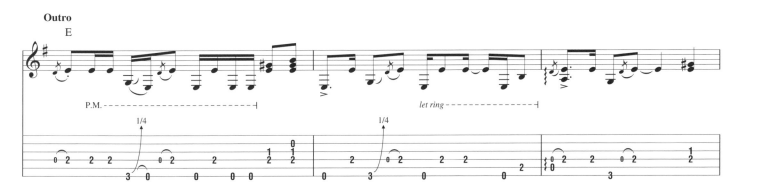

*Notes are sounded by slapping pick-hand
  index finger on fretboard.

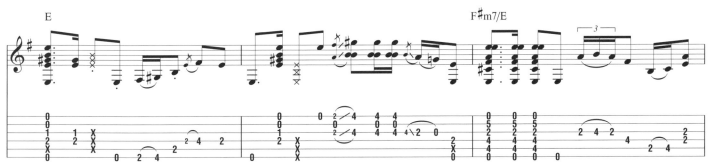

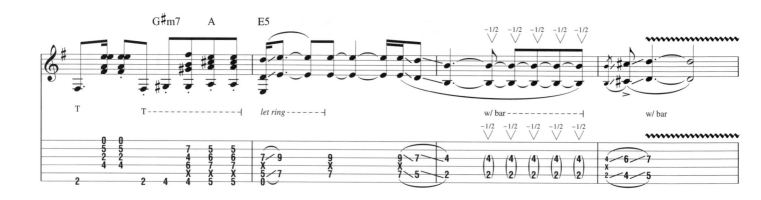

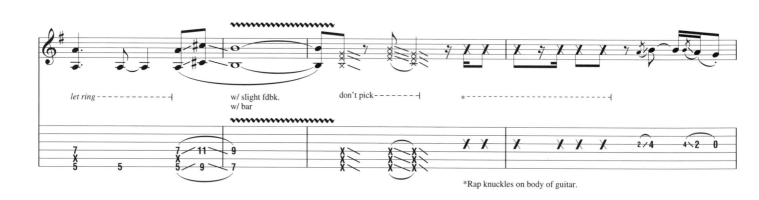

*Rap knuckles on body of guitar.

**Jimi checks his tuning.

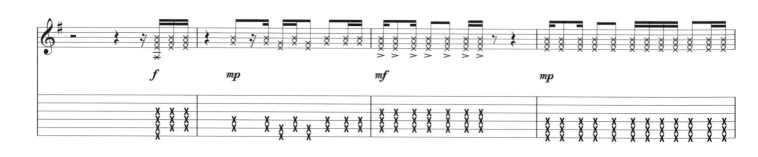

Segue to "In From the Storm"

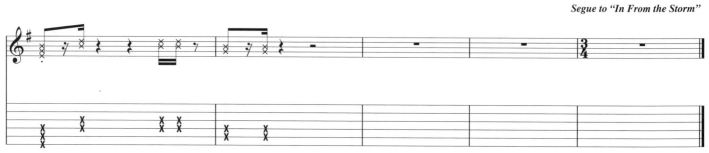

In From the Storm

Words and Music by Jimi Hendrix

Tune down 1/2 step:
(low to high) E♭-A♭-D♭-G♭-B♭-E♭

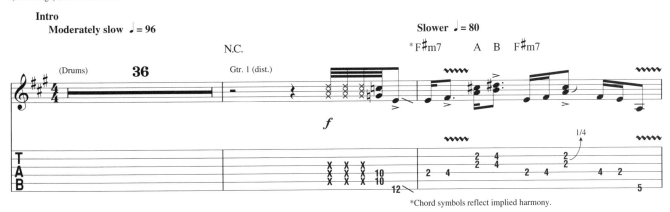

*Chord symbols reflect implied harmony.

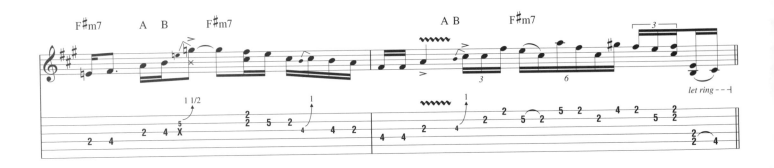

It was so cold an' lone - ly,

cry - in' blue rain was tear - in' me up!

Thank you, pret - ty ba - by,

let ring

let ring

for dig - gin' in the grave an' pick - in' me up!

8va *loco*

Harm.

*T

let ring

T = Thumb on 6th string

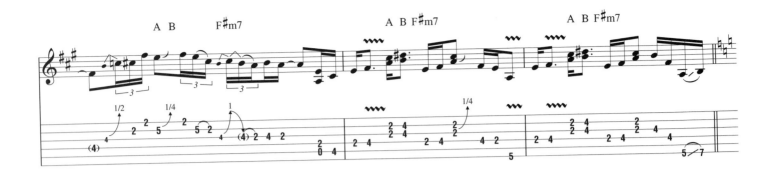

Interlude

Double time ♩ = 160

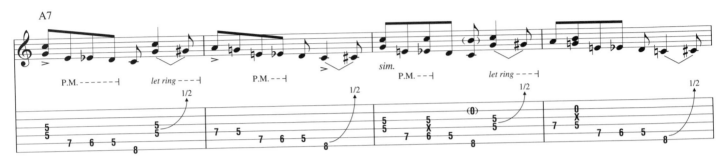

Guitar Solo

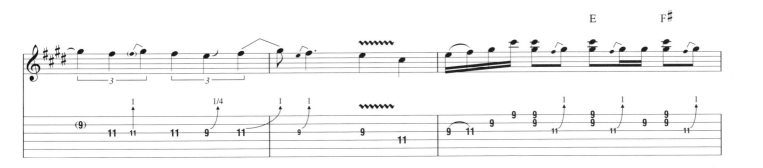

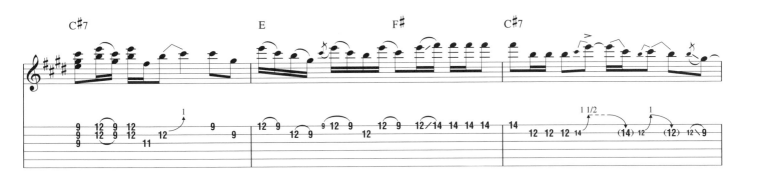

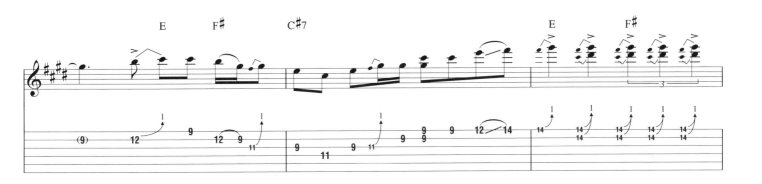

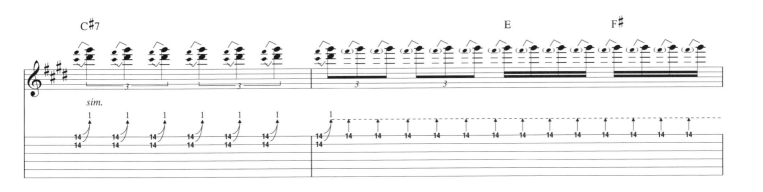

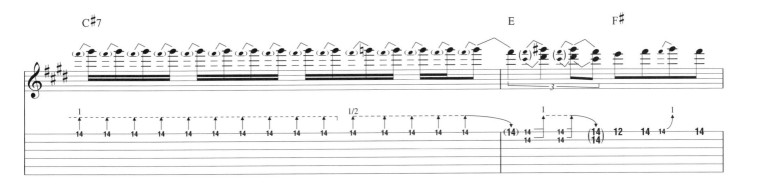

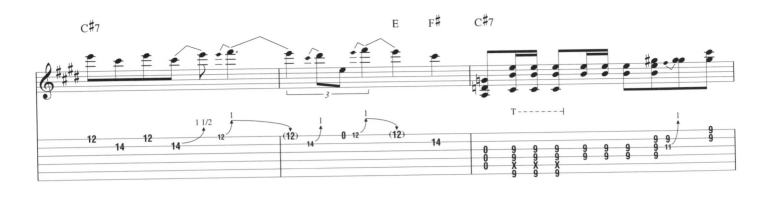

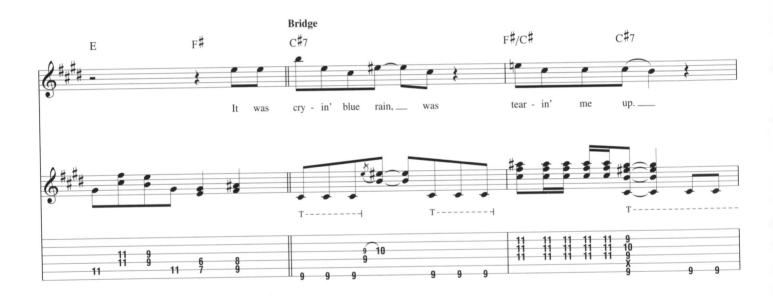

Outro

Half-time ♩ = 80

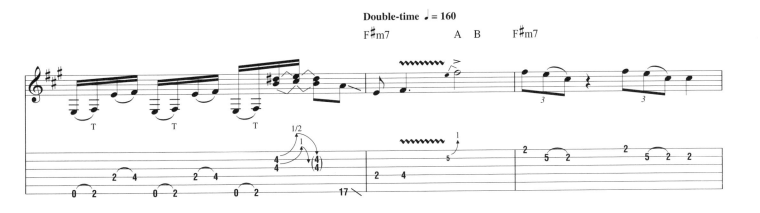

Double-time ♩ = 160

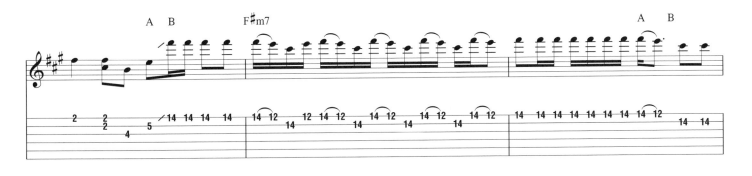

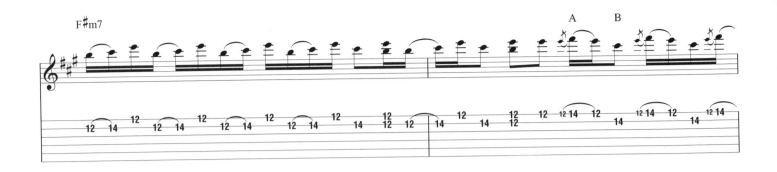

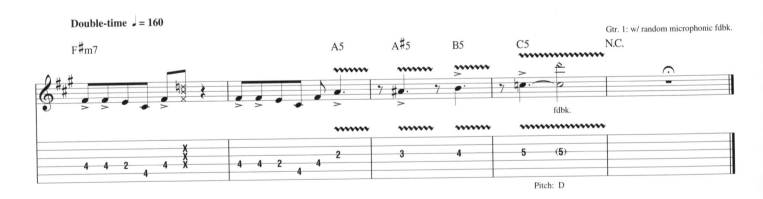

Spoken Farewell: *"Thank you for being so patient. Maybe one of these days we'll, uh, join again. I really hope so. Alright? Thank you very much, and peace and happiness and all that other good shit."*

Guitar Notation Legend

Guitar Music can be notated three different ways: on a *musical staff*, in *tablature*, and in *rhythm slashes*.

RHYTHM SLASHES are written above the staff. Strum chords in the rhythm indicated. Use the chord diagrams found at the top of the first page of the transcription for the appropriate chord voicings. Round noteheads indicate single notes.

THE MUSICAL STAFF shows pitches and rhythms and is divided by bar lines into measures. Pitches are named after the first seven letters of the alphabet.

TABLATURE graphically represents the guitar fingerboard. Each horizontal line represents a a string, and each number represents a fret.

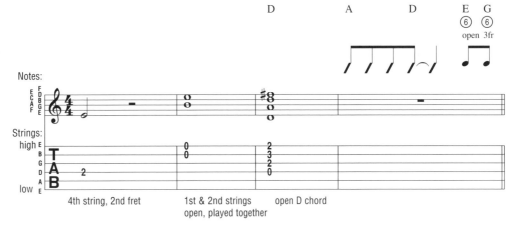

4th string, 2nd fret

1st & 2nd strings open, played together

open D chord

Definitions for Special Guitar Notation

HALF-STEP BEND: Strike the note and bend up 1/2 step.

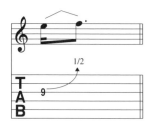

WHOLE-STEP BEND: Strike the note and bend up one step.

GRACE NOTE BEND: Strike the note and immediately bend up as indicated.

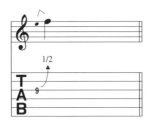

SLIGHT (MICROTONE) BEND: Strike the note and bend up 1/4 step.

BEND AND RELEASE: Strike the note and bend up as indicated, then release back to the original note. Only the first note is struck.

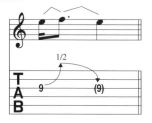

PRE-BEND: Bend the note as indicated, then strike it.

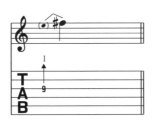

PRE-BEND AND RELEASE: Bend the note as indicated. Strike it and release the bend back to the original note.

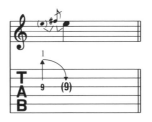

UNISON BEND: Strike the two notes simultaneously and bend the lower note up to the pitch of the higher.

VIBRATO: The string is vibrated by rapidly bending and releasing the note with the fretting hand.

WIDE VIBRATO: The pitch is varied to a greater degree by vibrating with the fretting hand.

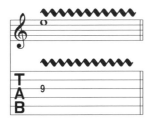

HAMMER-ON: Strike the first (lower) note with one finger, then sound the higher note (on the same string) with another finger by fretting it without picking.

PULL-OFF: Place both fingers on the notes to be sounded. Strike the first note and without picking, pull the finger off to sound the second (lower) note.

LEGATO SLIDE: Strike the first note and then slide the same fret-hand finger up or down to the second note. The second note is not struck.

SHIFT SLIDE: Same as legato slide, except the second note is struck.

TRILL: Very rapidly alternate between the notes indicated by continuously hammering on and pulling off.

TAPPING: Hammer ("tap") the fret indicated with the pick-hand index or middle finger and pull off to the note fretted by the fret hand.

NATURAL HARMONIC: Strike the note while the fret-hand lightly touches the string directly over the fret indicated.

Harm.

PINCH HARMONIC: The note is fretted normally and a harmonic is produced by adding the edge of the thumb or the tip of the index finger of the pick hand to the normal pick attack.

P.H.

HARP HARMONIC: The note is fretted normally and a harmonic is produced by gently resting the pick hand's index finger directly above the indicated fret (in parentheses) while the pick hand's thumb or pick assists by plucking the appropriate string.

H.H.

PICK SCRAPE: The edge of the pick is rubbed down (or up) the string, producing a scratchy sound.

P.S.

MUFFLED STRINGS: A percussive sound is produced by laying the fret hand across the string(s) without depressing, and striking them with the pick hand.

PALM MUTING: The note is partially muted by the pick hand lightly touching the string(s) just before the bridge.

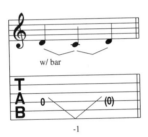

P.M.

RAKE: Drag the pick across the strings indicated with a single motion.

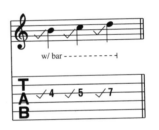

rake

TREMOLO PICKING: The note is picked as rapidly and continuously as possible.

ARPEGGIATE: Play the notes of the chord indicated by quickly rolling them from bottom to top.

VIBRATO BAR DIVE AND RETURN: The pitch of the note or chord is dropped a specified number of steps (in rhythm) then returned to the original pitch.

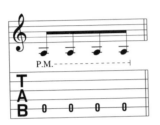

w/ bar

-1

VIBRATO BAR SCOOP: Depress the bar just before striking the note, then quickly release the bar.

w/ bar

VIBRATO BAR DIP: Strike the note and then immediately drop a specified number of steps, then release back to the original pitch.

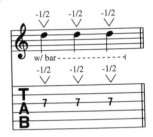

w/ bar

Additional Musical Definitions

(accent)	• Accentuate note (play it louder)	
(accent)	• Accentuate note with great intensity	
(staccato)	• Play the note short	
⊓	• Downstroke	
∨	• Upstroke	

Rhy. Fig. • Label used to recall a recurring accompaniment pattern (usually chordal).

Riff • Label used to recall composed, melodic lines (usually single notes) which recur.

Fill • Label used to identify a brief melodic figure which is to be inserted into the arrangement.

Rhy. Fill • A chordal version of a Fill.

tacet • Instrument is silent (drops out).

D.S. al Coda • Go back to the sign (𝄋), then play until the measure marked "*To Coda,*" then skip to the section labelled "*Coda.*"

D.C. al Fine • Go back to the beginning of the song and play until the measure marked "*Fine*" (end).

• Repeat measures between signs.

• When a repeated section has different endings, play the first ending only the first time and the second ending only the second time.

NOTE: Tablature numbers in parentheses mean:
1. The note is being sustained over a system (note in standard notation is tied), or
2. The note is sustained, but a new articulation (such as a hammer-on, pull-off, slide or vibrato begins), or
3. The note is a barely audible "ghost" note (note in standard notation is also in parentheses).